INSPIRATIONAL LESSONS FROM
THE WORLD'S FINEST SPORTS STARS

Jeff Grout & Sarah Perrin

Foreword by Sir Clive Woodward, OBE

CAPSTONE

First published in 2004 by Capstone Publishing Limited (a Wiley Company), The Atrium, Southern Gate, Chichester, West Sussex, PO19 8SQ, England. Phone (+44) 1243 779777

Email (for orders and customer service enquires): cs-books@wiley.co.uk
Visit our Home Page on www.wiley.co.uk or www.wiley.com

Other Wiley Editorial Offices

John Wiley & Sons Inc. 111 River Street, Hoboken, NJ 07030, USA
Jossey-Bass, 989 Market Street, San Francisco, CA 94103-1741, USA
Wiley-VCH Verlag GmbH, Pappellaee 3, D-69469 Weinheim, Germany
John Wiley & Sons Australia Ltd, 42 McDougall Street, Milton, Queensland 4064, Australia
John Wiley & Sons (Asia) Pte Ltd, 2 Clementi Loop #02-01, Jin Xing Distripark, Singapore 129809
John Wiley & Sons Canada Ltd, 22 Worcester Road, Etobicoke, Ontario, Canada, M9W 1L1

Wiley also publishes its books in a variety of electronic formats. Some content that appears in print may not be available in electronic books.

Library of Congress Cataloging-in-Publication Data is available
British Library Cataloguing in Publication Data
A catalogue record for this book is available from the British Library

ISBN 1-84112-739-6

Typeset in 10/12 pt Dutch 801 by Sparks, Oxford – www.sparks.co.uk

This book is printed on acid-free paper responsibly manufactured from sustainable forestry in which at least two trees are planted for each one used for paper production.

CONTENTS

FOREWORD BY
SIR CLIVE WOODWARD OBE

THE MENTAL SIDE OF SPORT is massive.

Before setting off to Australia for the 2003 World Cup I said that the competition would be won 'in the head'. It isn't necessarily the best team or the team with the most talented players that wins games, but the team that can 'think correctly under pressure': T-Cup for short. It's what's between the ears that counts.

This T-Cup ability separates out the true champions from the rest. Martin Johnson, Lawrence Dallaglio, Jonny Wilkinson, along with the rest of the team, don't panic under pressure. They think correctly and make the right decisions about what to do. When the England squad seized victory in the closing minutes of the World Cup final, the whole team had proved it could make the right decisions under the greatest pressure imaginable.

The great mental strength showed by the England team didn't just happen by chance. It was the result of sustained mental preparation during training.

The England team's success has also come by setting challenging goals. I have always aimed high, setting goals for myself throughout my playing career. As England's first full-time professional coach, I set one simple goal: for England to be the best team in the world.

The England team truly believed we could win the World Cup – and we did. That self-belief came as the result of a lot of hard work – repetitive training routines, meticulous preparation, attention to detail and mental rehearsal.

We also work as one team. Winning the World Cup resulted from the combined efforts of all players and all members of the coaching team. None of us could have achieved that result without the others. The England squad draws strength from a combination of leadership and 'teamship'. Leadership is about communicating an inspiring vision of the future, stimulating change, setting clear and measurable objectives and clearly communicating what is required from each individual. Teamship acknowledges the vital importance of peer pressure and peer approval, and that team decision-making encourages commitment and greater motivation to work hard.

Our shared attention to detail has proven invaluable. We use any and all information that can help us. If we can improve one hundred things by 1%, the total impact is huge. We embrace new ideas from any source in our efforts to maximize team performance.

The England rugby team's path to World Cup victory was not without its setbacks. Champions learn from their mistakes and grow stronger as a result. They don't feel inhibited by the fear of failure, but are stimulated and motivated by it. They also learn from their successes. With the England team I pay more attention to understanding the causes of our successes than our failures. It is the successes that we want to replicate.

Mind Games draws on the experiences of elite sportspeople, from many sports, focusing on the mental techniques they use to perform at their best.

Sir Clive Woodward OBE

ABOUT THE AUTHORS

Jeff Grout is an adviser, commentator and columnist on the subjects of motivation, peak performance, people management, teamwork, recruitment and retention. He is also business manager to Sir Clive Woodward OBE.

SARAH PERRIN is a freelance journalist and writer, contributing regularly to business and professional magazines. She is co-author of *Kickstart Your Career* and *Recruiting Excellence*, and author of *The Guardian Careers Guide to Accountancy*. She is also a qualified NLP practitioner, a technique increasingly used by sporting champions.

ACKNOWLEDGEMENTS

WE COULD NOT HAVE WRITTEN THIS BOOK without the help of many people. In particular we would like to thank Renzie Hanham and Ceri Evans from Gazing Performance, mental conditioning specialists. Their willingness not only to explain the Gazing approach, but also to comment on our own findings and analysis, proved invaluable. A special thank you also goes to sports psychologist Professor Graham Jones from Lane4, a specialist human performance consultancy, for sharing his research and insights. We are also indebted to sports psychologist Ian Lynagh, who helped us to develop our initial research plans and whose enthusiasm was inspiring.

We would also like to thank the following for their generous help in sharing their experiences for this book:

- Sir Clive Woodward OBE, former England rugby head coach
- Sven-Göran Eriksson, England football coach
- Matthew Pinsent CBE, rower, three times Olympic gold medallist
- Nick Faldo MBE, Britain's most successful golfer
- Ellen MacArthur MBE, fastest woman to sail around the world single-handed
- Steve Backley OBE, three times European and Commonwealth gold medallist and Olympic silver medallist in the javelin
- Roger Black MBE, 4 × 400m relay World Champion and Olympic silver medallist
- Jonny Wilkinson MBE, England rugby fly-half, arguably the world's best kicker
- David Platt, former Aston Villa, Sampdoria, Arsenal and England footballer and former manager of England's Under-21 team
- Sally Gunnell OBE, former Olympic, World, Commonwealth and European 400m hurdles champion
- Dr Stephanie Cook MBE, Olympic and World modern pentathlon champion
- Lawrence Dallaglio MBE, England rugby captain
- Ron Dennis CBE, boss of the McLaren Formula One motor racing team
- Howard Wilkinson, former Sunderland and Leeds United manager and former Football Association technical director
- David Lloyd, former Davis Cup captain
- Michael Lynagh, former Australian rugby captain
- Lord Coe OBE, former double Olympic 1500m champion
- Sir Chay Blyth CBE, round-the-world yachtsman
- Jack Charlton OBE, former England footballer and Ireland manager
- Gill Clark MBE, former European badminton doubles champion

- Adrian Moorhouse MBE, former Olympic 100m breast-stroke champion
- Mark Richardson, 400m Commonwealth silver medallist
- John Regis MBE, former European 200m and 4 × World 400m relay World Champion
- Richard Dunwoody MBE, record-breaking champion National Hunt jockey
- Ron Roddan, athletics coach (including coach of Linford Christie)
- Frank Dick OBE, former national athletics coach
- John Syer, sports psychologist to Tottenham Hotspur
- Graham Shaw, Neuro-Linguistic Programming (NLP) trainer
- Steve Sylvester, sports psychologist

INTRODUCTION

GERMANY 1:ENGLAND 5

THIS SCORELINE IN THE RUN UP to the 2002 World Cup remains a cause of joy and wonder for many an English football fan. It offered the bright promise of England regaining its long-awaited place at the top of international football.

That historic September 2001 World Cup qualifier against Germany was England's seventh match – and sixth win – under Sven-Göran Eriksson's leadership. Even more astoundingly, the England team achieved their triumphant result away from home, in Munich. The previous time England had played Germany, in October 2000, was also the last time Kevin Keegan sat in the manager's seat; on that occasion England was shamed at Wembley, defeated by one goal to nil.

So what made the difference in that one year gap? Commentators were desperate to know what magic Sven-Göran Eriksson had worked to transform Keegan's lacklustre side into this magnificent goal-scoring machine. After all, he had essentially the same set of players to select from and work with. So how had he done it? Sven's response when questioned was: 'First you must start with the head.'

That comment provided the initial inspiration for this book. Since then the England rugby team's triumphant victory in the 2003 World Cup in Australia, under the transformational leadership of Sir Clive Woodward, has stimulated further debate about what creates success in the sporting arena.

These inspirational wins fired our curiosity. We wanted to answer the question, what makes a champion? Why do some people consistently break records, cross the line first or hammer the ball into the net with pinpoint accuracy? Natural talent, regular training and fitness are obviously vital. But with two equally matched sportspeople, something else makes the difference and provides that champion factor – and that extra something is the mind.

Mind Games sets out to identify the mental characteristics that really differentiate a champion from the 'also rans'.

On our exploration we have called on the first-hand experiences of acknowledged champions from a range of sports. By talking to them about their attitudes and approaches to their sporting activities, we have tried to highlight common themes that apply to them all. We consider their beliefs, motivations and the training they do on the mental aspect of their games. We relive moments of high pressure – when a rugby match hung on one kick, when a gold medal depended on an explosive, focused race to the line. How do sports stars control their nerves, channel their adrenalin and deliver a peak performance on cue?

Sally Gunnell, one of the many champions we interviewed, had no hesitation in stating that the mental side of her performance made 'the difference between silver and gold'.

Celebrated yachtswoman Ellen MacArthur believes that mental strength, particularly determination, is an essential ingredient of any successful, competitive sailor: 'It's crucial. You can have the best boat in the world, but if you don't have the determination to finish the race, you may as well not start it. Determination counts for more than it's given credit for.'

David Platt, former England footballer and World Cup scorer, and former coach of the England Under-21 squad, acknowledges that top players have to have talent and skills. But he says: 'Mental strength is a major, major factor. They have to be ruthless; they have to be arrogant; they have to believe they are the best.'

In addition to the champions themselves, our research has also led us to sports psychologists, coaches and specialists in human behaviours. We have tapped into their expertise to identify some of the techniques that elite sportsmen and women use to strengthen their mental armoury, whether through visualization or mental rehearsal, or simply by setting ever more specific goals.

Coaches such as Frank Dick, who helped many top international athletes achieve repeated success, know how important an individual's mental outlook or attitude is to delivering winning performances. Dick says:

> 'I think 70% or 80% is about attitude. Once you've made sure that everybody's prepared for the task, it's just that – it's an attitude. The good news in life is that you can choose that. You can't always choose or change the circumstances in your arena, but you can always choose or change your attitude.'

Our aim in writing this book is partly to offer insights into the techniques that sporting champions use to deliver their best performance when they need it. However, the insights and techniques identified here are not only valuable in the sporting sphere; they also have relevance to other areas of all our lives.

Ian Lynagh, Australian sports psychologist, and father of Australia's greatest ever fly-half – Michael Lynagh – certainly believes that sport provides a framework for personal development. Sport appeals to people because it meets a basic, instinctive need to want to take on challenges and succeed, and it encourages them to develop skills along the way.

'It's the challenge of wanting to conquer and establish control over a task. It becomes an internal challenge. Sport, at its ultimate meaning for human beings, provides us with a structure which is helpful in growing as a person. It doesn't have to be sport. If it's not sport it might be climbing a mountain or running round a country. The human race has always done this – "Let's challenge ourselves to do something that's really difficult, that requires a lot of skill development, physical and mental development and also challenges us to overcome our weaknesses as a human being." By doing it we become a better person. To me, that's the ultimate meaning of doing sport.'

Rising to the mental challenge is an essential requirement for success in all endeavours, sporting or otherwise. The techniques that proven champions use can help us all, in any situation, where peak performance is a desired goal. Controlling your nerves, developing greater belief and visualizing your success can have a positive impact on activities as diverse as making a best man's speech or improving your team leadership skills at work.

Ron Dennis, the boss of the McLaren racing team, sums up our view of the importance of mental strength perfectly. If he, and we, are right, then using any techniques we can to improve our mental strength can only be a great benefit not only to ourselves, but to those with whom we live and work. As Dennis says:

'Life is a mind game. Every relationship you have is a mind game. Where does anger, tranquillity, happiness come from? They all come from your mind. In the end everything feeds into your mind, and everything starts from your mind. If you decide to be a muscular person your mind takes the decision to do the work to be a specific athlete. If you want

to be a successful athlete or a businessman, it all starts and finishes with the mind. Life is a mind game.'

Eriksson understands this supremely well.

'In football, it's difficult to do more in terms of physical, tactical or technical areas. But where you can do a lot more is in terms of mental work. In football I think we are behind other sports, such as tennis. Mental training is the future for football.'

We hope *Mind Games* inspires you to raise your game, whether in sport, your work or your personal life. The champions we met have achieved amazing feats, but they believe their success owes more to their mental strength than their natural talent. We can all learn from them and improve our own personal performances – increasing the enjoyment and satisfaction we gain from life as a result.

Part I
PERSONALITY POWER

Chapter 1

TRUE GRIT

WHAT DOES IT TAKE TO BE A CHAMPION? Talent, certainly. But talent isn't enough to be a world-beater. In sport, as in other areas of life, personal characteristics and mental qualities make the difference between repeated success and failure, between taking a champion's title and finishing in the last four.

These characteristics – the desire to win, the ability to learn from failure, the willingness to try new techniques, to name a few – arise time and again in the elite sportsmen and women who have managed to maintain their form over repeated competitions. Such personal features are considered throughout this book. First up for examination is the requirement for discipline and determination, a touch of selfishness and the essential killer instinct.

EARLY DISCIPLINE

Champions generally have to start training at a young age. That means they often show a natural sense of discipline.

Ellen MacArthur surged to fame when she became the fastest woman and the youngest person ever to circumnavigate the earth in a single-handed race, completing the 2001 Vendée Globe in second place. MacArthur is dedication personified. So strong was her passion for sailing that she made sacrifices to support her activity throughout her childhood.

'When I was about 14 I was already thinking about trying to save up my money for a small boat that I could live on as well as sail on the coast. My first boat was a little 8-foot dinghy, but you can't really live on a boat like that and I really fancied the idea of travelling places and having something that you could live on and cruise around in. In fact, I'd been saving up since the age of 8. Saving for a boat was a massive goal, which is why for lunch at school I'd have either nothing, or soup which cost 4 pence from the soup machine, or mashed potato and baked beans which cost a total of 8 pence. I saved everything because we didn't get pocket money as kids and birthdays and Christmases were quite spaced out, so it was basically about making savings every day.'

Adrian Moorhouse, Olympic gold medallist in the breaststroke in Seoul in1988, showed early dedication in the training regime he adopted as a youngster.

'I was pretty focused as a kid. I was training seven times a week at the age of 11. I'm a routine person, so if I know where I've got to be – the pool at a certain time – I'll get into the routine. I'm a very habitual person. I'll be there, I'll do it and I'll work hard.'

Sir Chay Blyth's achievements include becoming the first man to sail around the world against the prevailing winds and currents in 1971, for which he was awarded the CBE. Five years before that he broke the record for rowing across the Atlantic with British Army Captain John Ridgeway, completing the 3000-mile test of endurance in 92 days.

Blyth describes himself as having been 'a wild young boy', but he was also one with great capacity for discipline, as his childhood experiences show. That youngster was so inspired by a chance encounter with an Olympic swimmer that he took up swimming and embarked on a demanding training schedule.

'Through his encouragement I took up swimming and ended up training three times a day. I was 10 or 11. We lived about two and a half miles from the swimming baths and I would get up and run down there at 7 o'clock in the morning and then train, and then go to school, then come back at lunch time, and then go back in the evenings. Training three times a day must have taken quite a lot of determination – to be able to do that at that young age.'

It is just this kind of determination that was to support Blyth during the planning and execution of his epic voyages.

Chris Evert, who won three Wimbledon titles and a total of 18 Grand Slams, certainly trained hard as a youngster. She was drilled by her father to practise shots over and over again, hitting forehands and backhands down every line of the court. These early years contributed hugely to her tennis success as an adult. The training approach was quite different to that used by the young Lloyd brothers, David and John, who weren't drilled to hit the same shot so repeatedly. John particularly showed huge natural talent, but perhaps didn't have the absolute discipline required to make it right to the top of the game. David says:

'John realized that practice would make him good, which he wanted to be. But sometimes he would say, "Ugh, I can't practise today; it's too hot." Or it would be too windy. Therefore he didn't follow through. Becoming a champion

*definitely requires a control of your mind, and it's very
important to be able to learn that at a very young age.'*

David Lloyd believes that aspiring tennis champions need to
understand that what they do on the practice court has direct
bearing on how they will do in matches. They learn their
matchplay on the practice court. Therefore, coaches look for
kids with the ability to practise consistently well, day after day
– like Tim Henman did as a youngster. When Lloyd worked
with him between the ages of 12 and 16, he never put in a bad
day's practice.

JUGGLING DEMANDS AND MAKING CHOICES

Dr Stephanie Cook, who took the gold medal in the modern
pentathlon in the 2000 Sydney Olympics, knows all about discipline. Before becoming a full-time sportswoman she initially
maintained her training regime while working as a junior
doctor. This was in the days before modern pentathlon was
even an Olympic event for women, so she didn't even have the
inspiration of winning one of the sporting world's glittering
prizes to spur her on.

> *'If ever I'm doing something I will always try and put 100%
> into it. It doesn't have to be sport. I always try to do the best
> I can. That was a driving factor behind me doing well in the
> modern pentathlon.*
>
> *'I think my determination showed when it involved get-
> ting up at 5.30am to go swimming before going to work. As
> a junior doctor I was running around all day, so was abso-
> lutely shattered after work. But then I'd get home, put my
> kit on, go out for a run or sit in the car and drive for an hour
> to go fencing, and then come back. You're absolutely shat-
> tered. I did that because I loved it, because I got more out of
> my life, and I got more out of my job by doing that – but so
> many people thought I was completely crazy. I didn't know
> many other people who would actually do what I did and
> go to the lengths that I went to at that time.'*

Once it seemed likely that the women's modern pentathlon would be made an Olympic event, Cook finally opted for the easier option of giving up her job to train full-time with the backing of lottery funding: 'I could sleep properly and eat properly and I wasn't rushing off to go to work. It was great,' she says.

Even when champions are established stars in their field, there are no shortcuts in terms of the hours of training required – hours that are often unsociable. Three times Olympic champion Matthew Pinsent starts rowing on the Thames at 7.30 in the morning. Does he ever ask himself why he's doing it? Yes, he certainly does – most mornings. Training for four years just to win one race – Olympic gold – isn't easy. He knows it is inevitable that there will be some bad days, as well as the good ones.

His training routine puts him out of step with most people's daily lives. He may get some time to himself that other people would be spending at work, but the strange hours aren't easy.

'Today we finished around 1 o'clock – that's a lot earlier than anyone else. So I get this afternoon and evening to do whatever I want and then come back tomorrow and do some more. It is a different routine to everyone else in life, which is kind of tough. You lose your weekends too.'

Nevertheless, Pinsent has sufficient reserves of discipline and dedication to keep turning up at the river for more training.

'Part of it is simply knowing that there are going to be bad days. You just have to accept that there is no one in life who gets out of bed every morning thinking "Yeah, great, hooray", whatever job they do, however much they love it. But compared to 99% of the population … I love my job more than most.'

Former badminton champion Gill Clark accepted the commitment she made to her sport because she alone had decided this was what she wanted to do with her life. She doesn't think it appropriate for people to talk about having to make 'sacrifices'. What top performers do is make 'choices'. Clark stresses that she chose to concentrate her efforts on developing her sporting career – it was a conscious decision to put other things to the side and make badminton her priority.

This choice wasn't necessarily an easy one. In Clark's experience her commitment to competitive badminton at the highest level made it hard to maintain personal relationships.

> 'I was forever on the road. It's not as bad as for tennis players, but you're on the road. Whilst it's getting better, it's still not really accepted that the woman travels and leaves the man at home, and he's got to do the laundry and cook for himself and all those sort of things. It's quite all right for a man to do that, to travel on business, but it's still not really acceptable for a woman. The other thing is, if you're deeply in love, and I'm flying off to Taipei and Japan and Korea, and I'm going to be away for three and a half weeks, you start missing him. So then, because you have all these negative emotions, it impacts your performance. Therefore, I made the choice that that was all going to have to be put on hold.'

RESOLVE, PIG-HEADEDNESS AND COMMITMENT

Ron Dennis, boss of the McLaren racing team, has had plenty of experience in assessing what it is that makes a top quality Formula One racing driver. The vital ingredient for him is 'steely resolve'.

> 'You can often see if someone has got what it takes. It's not when discussing with someone whether they should join your team, but when they are under stress and being pushed to succeed that you see their resolve. In our sport there are many drivers who are capable of winning races and world championships in the best car, but you rarely have a situation where the car is the best all the time. It's how the driver finds it in himself to make up for the performance deficien-

cies of the car. It comes from their resolve and if they want to succeed.'

David Lloyd certainly has great belief in the power of determination, which he applies in his business life. He likens the challenges you meet in sport and general life to an enormous wall. If there isn't an easy way through, you have to continue to find a way to get past the wall – even if it means making a compromise.

> *'Walls will come down all the time in everything you do – bloody high walls. When one does, you've got to get over it. If you can climb it, terrific; if you can't climb it, walk around it. You might have to compromise to get around the other side, but if you don't get around the side, you're dead anyway. You may have to compromise in tennis in the way you're hitting the ball; in business you may have to compromise on giving away a little bit more of the deal. But you've got to get around the other side of that wall.'*

Sebastian Coe's talent and dedication took him to the top of the athletic world, twice winning the Olympic 1500 metres. He also once held the 800 metres, 1000 metres, 1500 metres and one-mile records simultaneously. Coe's success depended in part on his amazing natural talent, but he couldn't have achieved such sporting heights without a lot of hard work and commitment.

> *'Without getting boring and scientific about it, I do have a very low heart rate; I have a very large oxygen ability for oxygen uptake … I have a light frame and I always ran in balance. That was the luck of the draw. I don't think that in itself would have been enough to get me beyond being a useful national standard competitor. The difference between that and getting onto a rostrum for major championships is 80 miles a week, ten to twelve hours in the gym and all the other things that go with it.*
>
> *'There are plenty of athletes I have worked with – you can see them from relatively young ages – who*

precocious talent but fall through the net. Sometimes that's because they just are not prepared mentally to commit to it. If they are not prepared to do that then they will be much happier going off to do something else. There is nothing worse than seeing people in sport at 14, 15 and 16 being pushed into something that really doesn't interest them and they don't want to commit to it.'

England fly-half Jonny Wilkinson derives confidence and belief from the work he puts in practising kicks. The training gives him greater confidence when preparing for a difficult kick, or one with the potential to win the game. He believes he 'deserves' success because of all the hard work he has put in when training; his dedication gives him the right to succeed. He knows that natural talent can count for a great deal of a player's achievements, but the harder an individual works, the better he will get. Certainly, the ability to put in a consistently good performance, rather than just a one-off stunt, relies on dedicated practice. Top athletes have to make a personal investment in time and effort if they want to improve their chances of being successful when the pressure is on.

Wilkinson had this realization that training hard is the best route to consistency when he was 16.

'Some days I was great and some days I was terrible. I went to see the team coach and I realized that it wasn't about having a gift, about having good and bad days that you weren't in control of. There was something you could do to improve your chances of getting the ball over. If you practised hard and did the right things, you could have good days every day. Now I won't ever go into a situation where I'm not prepared. Any kick I miss, I can explain everything about why I missed.'

termination to win against an aggressive opposition is the
k of a top quality rugby team. England captain Lawrence
glio recalls the battle between England and France in
hen the England squad were playing away from home

'We had a number of opportunities in that game to give ourselves a comfortable lead, but we didn't take them. As a result, there was always going to come a time when the French were going to come back at us – and they did. It ended up being real "backs-to-the-wall" stuff, but the character of the England players came through.

'The match ended with the French peppering the English line, but it was a line that was firm. There's a great photo which shows it – a line of Englishmen repelling a French attack and they are all glowering at the French.'

England held on to win 15–9.

For round-the-world yachtswoman Ellen MacArthur, determination is essential if she is to survive the extreme demands she makes of herself. For example, sleep deprivation is the norm. Before competing in the Vendée Globe for the first time, MacArthur sailed her then newly built boat *Kingfisher* back from New Zealand to the UK. During the trip she analysed her sleep patterns.

'We studied when I slept naturally when I was at sea 24 hours a day. The weather has an impact, but generally speaking you can sleep when you want to. I learnt when I had the most tendency to sleep and therefore when I benefited most from it. Of course, at the end of the day a lot of your sleep is controlled by the weather and you have to sleep when you can. But the study showed me how much I slept in 24 hours. It's easy to lose track of that when you're on the boat. In the single-handed transatlantic race I slept for 4.2 hours in every 24 on average over two weeks.'

For MacArthur, this kind of knowledge was invaluable when trying to pace herself in long, solo races. She believes that being mentally aware of what state you are in is one of the biggest factors in determining success at sea. You simply can' give 100% for three days and then be exhausted if you a competing in a race lasting seven days. Pacing yourself, forc yourself to control your energy expenditure, is essential.

SELFISH STREAKS

If you're dedicated to winning, that may mean you need a degree of selfishness to get you onto the winner's podium.

Adrian Moorhouse, who fulfilled his dream of winning an Olympic gold medal in the breaststroke in 1988 in Seoul, certainly thinks so. Moorhouse admits that champions have to be so focused on what they are trying to achieve that 'you're not necessarily the nicest person to be around'.

> *'Being nice didn't matter when you wanted to win. You would be nice if you knew it would get you to where you wanted to get to, if it would contribute to your performance. They are not things I am proud of in hindsight, but I wasn't a nasty person. I know I was quite selfish. I mean, my mum has called me selfish. I think it's different in real life, particularly in business.'*

When racing solo Moorhouse didn't worry about being nice; he made good use of legal gamesmanship. If Moorhouse was ahead of one of his close rivals in a race, he would move over to swim at the side of his lane that was nearest to that rival. It was a move he knew might just give him the edge to win.

It may be that top champions need such dedication and focus on achieving their goals that they simply appear selfish. According to sports psychologist Professor Graham Jones, research shows that motivation, relating to mental toughness, falls into two dimensions. There is the determination to come back after failure, because the individual believes in themselves, but there are also internalized motives to succeed.

Jones says that lots of performers will talk about doing what they do in order to 'show' somebody, perhaps an ex-teacher who told them they would never amount to much; but underpinning that desire are really strong, internalized motives – the individual is really doing it for themselves. As Jones says, people don't train at 5 o'clock in the morning seven days a week just for the recognition they get for winning a gold medal.

Something else has to drive the person on – their personal sense of pride and satisfaction. This is why many elite performers can come across as selfish – because they know what they want to do, why they are doing it and they are not going to deviate or be distracted from that.

For some athletes, hurting those they are close to is part of the preparation for competition. Former national athletics coach Frank Dick recalls Daley Thompson's approach to the build-up:

> *'His preparation, eventually, was nothing to do with anyone other than himself. He took it upon himself in the run-in to a major championship to almost exercise his aggression on the people who were closest to him. He really was not easy to live with at those times. He'd worked out that if he could hurt the people who were closest to him, everybody else would be easy to handle in the arena.'*

KILLER INSTINCT

Winners seize their opportunities to win. They have an attitude that says 'take no prisoners'. David Platt, former coach of the England Under-21 squad and former England player, doesn't think players should have any feeling for the opposition. He can't understand why someone on a winning team might feel sorry for the losing side. He believes the better players don't really care. If his team is winning 3–0 at half time, Platt will challenge them to go out and win 6–0. They shouldn't think the game is over. Nor should they feel sorry for their opponents, but accept that it is the other side's fault they are losing so badly. Above all, they mustn't let them off the hook.

When football players don't give their all or let that killer instinct slip, there is a danger they will underperform. Take the England football team's apparent ability to raise their game when playing real threats – such as Germany or Argentina – but the tendency to crumble against lesser sides. England coach Sven-Göran Eriksson says:

*'It relates to the mental approach to the game. If you meet
Argentina or Germany, you know that the match will be
difficult and you must perform at your absolute best. When
you meet Macedonia at home, you think it will be okay.
So the mental approach to the games is different. But it's
not only England where that happens. I think it happens in
football in general.'*

Theoretically, a side should have a better record at home than
away, emboldened by the familiarity of the ground and the
home support. However, as 2002 drew to a close, Eriksson
noticed this didn't seem to be the case with England. Contrary
to expectation, England were doing better away than at home.
As he said, 'It's very strange'.

*'Maybe we think it's easy at home. When you think things
are easy, you are not prepared to kill your opponent, and so
you will never have a good result. You must have that killer
instinct. The ball is a 50:50 ball and you think, "That's my
ball".'*

For some sporting champions, competitions become almost
like real battles. Javelin champion Steve Backley likens
champions to 'warriors' and the experience of entering a competition to going into battle. Backley doesn't feel that he is
playing a game; he feels that he is 'fighting for my life'. In major
championships he convinces himself that it is a case of 'live or
die'. The event is, in a sense, blown out of all proportion in his
emotions.

Backley likens the contest between top javelin throwers to
a fight, with each throw a punch landed on the other. This was
how he saw his battle for silver in the 2000 Olympics, when
Backley was facing stiff competition from Sergei Makarov of
Russia.

*'I think he thought he'd beaten me and went to sleep. But
I had a response, and went ahead of him. Then he had a
chance to respond. In the fight analogy, it was as if I'd just*

squared him on the chin. It shook him a bit. He threw a
reasonable 86m, which made me think he was capable of
doing it, but he overcooked it. I caught him on the hop.'

In the end Backley threw 89.85m, a longer distance than
Makarov's best effort, so taking the silver and pushing the
Russian into the bronze medal position.

Having considered the discipline, determination and sometimes downright selfish pigheadedness shown by sporting
champions, we move on to consider some of the influences
that helped to make them what they are.

Chapter 2

I BELIEVE!

ONE OF THE CHARACTERISTICS THAT LEAPS OUT from most champion sportspeople is the depth and strength of their self-belief. That belief not only encourages them to keep training year after year, but helps them come back to form after injury and hold their nerve in the heat of competition.

BELIEF MATTERS

Professor Graham Jones has been researching the qualities of mental toughness that distinguish the truly elite performers from the rest. His studies of athletes have generated a ranking of qualities required for mental toughness. Self-belief has emerged as the top requirement, the most important characteristic of all.

Elite sportspeople from a range of disciplines, including swimming, sprinting, triathlon, golf and rugby, determined that this was the most important characteristic of mental toughness: 'Having an unshakable self-belief in your ability to achieve your competition goals.'

Belief also appeared in another form, ranked third in importance: 'Having an unshakable self-belief that you possess unique qualities and abilities that make you better than your opponents.' Champion athletes need to believe that they are better than the competition.

Whatever sport you look at, belief is essential. Ron Dennis, boss of the McLaren racing team, says: 'Ego is an essential ingredient in winners.'

In her competitive days, Olympic hurdler Sally Gunnell had a strong bond with top sprinter Linford Christie and hurdler Kriss Akabusi. What common characteristics did they all share?

> *'I guess it's believing in yourself. If you don't believe in yourself when you stand on the line, then you're not going to go anywhere. We believed in what we'd done, who we were and what we're made up of. We were all quite selfish people. When people know me I'm not a bitchy character. A lot of people used to say I'm like the girl next door, but I was someone very different as soon as I stepped onto that track.'*

Daley Thompson, Olympic gold medallist in the decathlon in 1980 and 1984, had huge self-belief, as former national athletics coach Frank Dick recalls:

> *'Just after a hard day's work, when we were sitting back and feeling the sun on our faces, Daley said to me, "Frankie, who's the greatest athlete you ever saw?" I asked if he meant even in videos, and he said yes. I named someone who had made four world records in one day. Daley said, "Forget it, buddy, you're looking at him".'*

DEVELOPING BELIEF

There clearly is no doubt that belief is an essential ingredient of champions, top athletes who can rise to major occasions and pull out medal-winning performances. The question is, where does that belief come from? Is it inherent or can it be developed?

According to sports psychologist, Steve Sylvester, the factors that enable champions to have rock-solid belief, and that therefore enable them to win consistently, are unique to each individual. This unique formula for strong belief is based on the individual's past experiences and how the person feels about the people around them. Sylvester notes that there are common ingredients that world champions exhibit, and the first one is the 'never say die' approach – the ability to work and persist in what they are doing, no matter what. The question he asks is, where does that come from? Is it innate? A lot of the people Sylvester works with persist for a combination of two reasons: because they *want* to achieve something (their dream), and because they *need* to achieve it.

For many top athletes, belief develops over time, as the individual meets and surpasses graduated goals. No one can give someone else belief in themselves, it has to be generated by each individual for themselves.

Frank Dick, former national athletics coach, says it is essential to give people the opportunity to build self-belief for themselves. He says:

'I cannot give you self-belief. This is a bridge that only you have to build and only you can cross. The self-belief comes from believing that you can explore, that you can challenge, that you can win. It's a growing thing, all the time. You've got to have "a guid conceit o' yersel".'

Hurdling gold medallist Sally Gunnell built up her confidence and belief little by little.

'I was OK as a junior, but I wasn't brilliant. I wasn't one of these people who went and won junior championships. But I was a confident athlete. If one year I got into a senior international, I gained a lot of confidence from it. Then I would set myself the next goal. I would just build up gradually like that. A lot of people talk about being Olympic champion one day. I was never really like that. I guess the first time I realized I could win the Olympics was about four years before it actually happened – when I was 15 in Seoul in 1988.'

For David Platt, former England player, belief in how high he could rise in the game of football developed gradually. Platt started out with Manchester United.

'I have always been a realist and I didn't actually think I was good enough to go to Manchester United. I signed a Youth Training Scheme [YTS] contract with them. I never trained with the first team, but every now and again we would have a practice match against them. You didn't believe you should be in the same building as them. To be awarded a pro contract at the end of that twelve months' YTS was fantastic. I was on cloud nine. But six months in I had the chance to go to Crewe Alexandra on loan. I knew I couldn't replace the likes of Norman Whiteside, Mark Hughes or Frank Stapleton at Manchester, so I went to Crewe. Even though it was a massive step down club-wise, it was a big step up in terms of the level of football I was going to be playing. I had been playing third team football at Manchester United and the odd reserve game. So to go and play league football was daunting. Even then you think you are not good enough to play in this and it takes a while to come to terms with it. Then you realize you are good enough to play, but you think maybe this is the highest you are going to go.'

Even when Aston Villa paid £200,000 – a huge fee at the time – to buy Platt from Crewe, he still doubted himself. Platt says:

> *'I had gone from being the big fish at Crewe to being with players who were top of the old second division. I began thinking maybe that was too much for me.'*

For Platt, absolute confidence in his own ability came some time after he first began playing first-class and international football. It was scoring a match-winning goal against Belgium in the 1990 World Cup in Italy that made the difference. The goal, right at the end of extra time, put England through to the quarter-finals.

> *'Scoring that goal in the World Cup put an expectancy level on me from everybody else. Scoring that goal in the last minute changed my life completely. I had already played ten or eleven times for England, but scoring that goal in the World Cup finals was something else. Afterwards I went to Hong Kong with Aston Villa. I got off the plane and there were thousands of people waiting to see me.*
>
> *'So then I had to keep delivering, and keep delivering, and keep delivering, and I did. After the World Cup I started to score at Aston Villa on a regular basis. I kept scoring goals at international level against good teams. And once you keep doing that you start thinking, "I can do this". And then you go week in, week out, and there is no fear inside you whatsoever. In fact, there's just an excitement level. It sounds horrible, but it's almost an arrogance. But as long as that arrogance is channelled in the right way, I don't think there's anything wrong with it. In fact, it's total confidence.'*

Platt's confidence fuelled itself as he kept scoring goals at international level, but he actively worked to reinforce it too:

> *'I had a video of all my goals that I would watch before I went out to play a game, because it made me feel good. They were good goals I had scored against good players.'*

For Jack Charlton too, belief in his ability came slowly. He was compared to his brother Bobby and always seen as less talented. Jack worked briefly in the mines before leaving home for Leeds United at the age of 16, where he was a member of the ground staff. At that time he describes himself as a five foot ten beanpole; thin with long legs – 'a gawky bugger'.

At the age of 17 the club decided whether it wanted to sign its youngsters. When Jack was 17, Leeds signed him up on the standard one-year contract, giving him a £10 signing fee and first team pay – about three and a half times what he had been earning on the ground staff.

> *'I walked out of the office and across to John's, a shop on the corner. John asked me if I had signed and I said "yes". John said, "Thank god for that." I asked why and he replied, "I have had half the Football League in here this morning to see if they had signed you. Scouts from all the clubs in the area and from all over the place have been in here asking about you. They all knew it was your birthday and they wanted to know if you had signed." I suddenly thought that I must be able to play.'*

Charlton enjoyed the feeling and began to absorb the fact that he really was a professional football player.

THAT 'KNOWING' FEELING

Some top sportsmen and women develop such a strong sense of belief that they feel they 'know' they will do well. This sense of knowing what the outcome will be results from absolute and unshakeable confidence in their abilities.

Multiple gold medal-winning rower Matthew Pinsent talks about 'knowing' how his boat should do in a race.

> *'I've been lucky enough in the Olympics to know that if the boat I was in rowed its best, we would win. That was the bedrock of it: "we are the best crew in the event and if we row well, we will win".'*

Olympic gold medal hurdler Sally Gunnell had an overwhelming sense of self-belief when standing on the start line before the Barcelona Olympic final.

> *'I remember standing on the line thinking, "I know I'm going to win this". I suppose I knew I was capable of winning it beforehand, but then I just knew. Something said to me, "You're going to win this".*
>
> *'I don't remember much of the race. I don't remember going over the first hurdle, second, third … Then I was at the eighth. A key thing I had done in visualizing the race was to say, "If I can be ahead at eight, I know I can win it," because I was stronger than the others. And then that was it – I was crossing the line.'*

Belief is generated in large part from knowing that everything has been done as well as it could be in preparation for the competition. Effective training builds up confidence, which leads to belief.

For Gunnell, having belief that she would win at the start of a race depended on her having trained well and knowing that she was in good shape.

> *'Confidence is everything. Thinking that I'd eaten no chocolate or whatever for six months just made me ooze confidence. Knowing that I hadn't had an injury gave me confidence. The mental side of it played the biggest part; that was the difference between silver and gold.'*

When Gunnell was injured in 1996 and missed training, she lost her sense of belief.

> *'I think of myself as mentally a very strong character, but I didn't do very well when I was injured. I had to be able to stand on the line knowing I was at my best.'*

Sebastian Coe believes that the mental aspect of success is huge, but he also sees a link with the physical.

'I always found I was mentally at my best when I was physically in good shape. If I knew I had run and trained and done everything I could possibly have done; if I knew I had left no stone unturned in training and had been uninjured and had a good, clear run through to a championship, then I was always mentally bouncy about it.

'If you are not in good shape, that is where good poker players take over. I have gone out onto the line before a race knowing that in reality the training had gone badly and that I was not in good shape. Maybe I had been injured. In poker terms you have a handful of crap, but you have got through it because you have maintained a mask. People think you're as good as you were six months ago. If you don't let them know you have been injured or out of form for a bit, then you can normally wing it a bit.'

Former England rugby head coach, Clive Woodward, believes really top sportsmen strive for every marginal advantage they can get. They build up their belief by knowing they are the fittest, the strongest, the sharpest – whatever it takes.

'Everybody is looking for the edge. It's getting smaller and smaller the more competitive the world of sport becomes. Take Tiger Woods. If someone asks him why he's better than the rest of the world, he talks about his fitness; he doesn't talk about his golf swing. He talks about feeling mentally stronger and that comes down to believing he's the fittest. He's an athlete. He's as fit as the 100m champion. He thinks he's fitter than any athlete in the world. He has massive mental strength.'

EXPECTATIONS SET BELIEF SETS REALITY

What an athlete believes can determine the outcome. There is no doubt that in sport as in many other areas of life, there is such a thing as the self-fulfilling prophecy. If you limit your beliefs, you limit your potential to achieve.

Steve Sylvester, sports psychologist, works with sportspeople and people in business to try to help them improve their self-belief. By talking to them and asking questions he brings to light what it is that is stopping someone achieving their goals. Nine times out of ten, people are blocking their own performance, Sylvester says. They stop themselves believing that they can achieve. He has found that when it comes to the critical match situations or key moments in games, what people choose to say to themselves really matters. That's what makes the difference between success or failure, winning or losing.

Nick Faldo had huge belief in himself and his ability to succeed in golf, even from a young age. He recalls going to his youth employment office when he was leaving school and being asked whether he was good with his hands and so on, in an attempt to identify suitable work.

> *'I said, "Excuse me, I'm going to be a pro golfer." They said, "No, no, only one in two thousand or ten thousand makes it." So I said, "Fine. I'm the one." I had that level of self-commitment.'*

Faldo's belief in himself developed gradually after he began going on tour. In the first four years he won roughly one tournament a year and he began wondering how he could win more. He realized that back on his first tour in South Africa, an influential person had told him he was good enough to win one tournament a year. And that's what he had done. Armed with that insight, and assisted by a psychologist, Faldo developed the belief that he could win multiple tournaments, which is precisely what he then started to do.

Athlete John Regis also knows that what you believe tends to come true. He recalls a Grand Prix race in Nice fairly early in his career. Also in the race were Frankie Fredericks, Michael Johnson and Linford Christie.

> *'I thought, "Michael's in the race, so I'm second." Then there was Frankie so I thought, "I haven't beaten him yet,*

so I'm third," and so on. I crossed the line fourth. It was a self-fulfilling prophecy because I told myself I was going to finish fourth. It was as if my body gauged it to finish fourth. It was a strange feeling. When the gun went bang I took off really well. I came off the straight and felt strong. Then Michael kicked and ran away a bit and Frankie kicked and ran away a bit, and then Linford kicked and ran away a bit. I thought it was my turn, but then all of a sudden it seemed my mind was saying, "No, leave it alone John, they're too good."

'Afterwards I sat down with my coach and he said it looked as though I was going to go, but I didn't. I told myself I would finish fourth, and I did.'

After that race Regis trained hard and his times improved. He realized he was good enough to be at least as good as the three who had beaten him. He began to feel he could win. As Regis says:

'If you believe you can, you have a chance. If you don't believe, you have no chance. Your mind can manipulate you from a no-win situation to a win-win situation.'

Regis recalls how he ran badly in a race in France, running a time of 20.9 seconds – what he calls a 'pedestrian, ugly' performance. Regis' coach then changed his training over the next week, making him focus on one area – really attacking the turn so hard that Regis worried it would use up too much energy. Despite Regis' concerns, they kept practising it all week. Eight days after his disastrous race, Regis competed in Lausanne. He ran the turn hard, as he had practised and finished in 20.1 seconds; he had knocked eight tenths of a second off his time in eight days.

'I'd improved eight and a half yards in seven days. It was huge. If you tell yourself you can, you can. All these little instances where I have overturned a negative and turned it into a positive helped me to perform at major champion-

ships and be more relaxed and just believe. You get yourself into shape no matter what anyone else is doing. Get yourself into shape and believe that you can. When it's your time to perform, it's your time to perform.'

BOUNCING BACK

Belief is essential not only when things are going well, but also when trying to recover from a setback.

Golfer Nick Faldo's belief was put to the test when he was already successful at the sport and European number one. Despite this, Faldo began to have doubts about his swing and decided to take some time out to improve his technique.

'I led the British Open in 1983 with nine holes to play at Birkdale and couldn't finish it off. The little voice began saying, "You ain't got it mate; you ain't got the next level." I was tinkering with my swing for a couple of years on my own and then I met David Leadbetter [a leading golf instructor] in Sun City at the end of 1984. I asked him what he thought of my swing and he gave me his view. I thought it made sense. I really struggled at the beginning of 1985 and started work with David in May 1985.'

Playing tournaments while trying to work on the swing proved extremely stressful for Faldo.

'The media's on you. You've gone from European number one and now your game's gone, so you're under pressure. It was brutal. I lost corporate deals. Just two companies stuck with me. Everybody else disappeared. My manager would come to the house bringing doom and gloom that someone else had gone. Your income's not happening.

'But I just kept going. I guess it was self-belief; every week saying, "Yes, I believe it's a little better this week." I'd go to the next tournament and believe I was doing the right thing. I remember seeing even the guys on the range mimicking me and thinking I'd lost the plot.'

Faldo carried on regardless and finally, in the spring of 1987, his swing clicked. He played at a B class tournament in Hattiesburg, Mississippi, and came second. Then he went to the Spanish Open and won. He finally began to believe he could win the British Open – The Open – and went to compete at Muirfield, in Scotland.

> *'I had all the right feelings that week. I knew something was going to happen. I actually had a premonition way back. In 1978 I played in The Open and finished four shots back in seventh. I said to myself, "I will win The Open one day".'*

Winning in 1987 required Faldo to contend with dreadful weather, as the Scottish fog closed in.

> *'I was nervous. I was trying to make birdies and I couldn't hole the putts. Then the East Lothian pea soup set in. Everything beyond a step and a half around me was out of focus. But I just kept plugging it out.'*

Faldo describes himself as 'cocooned' that week.

> *'I could see myself walking down the fairway. All I knew was that one great shot would win me that Open, and one bad shot would lose it.'*

As history shows, Faldo won.

There is no doubt that belief is a powerful element in the mixture of qualities that makes up a sporting champion. So is the ability to think positively about life and whatever happens to you, even if it doesn't initially seem that good. We examine this characteristic, one displayed by many elite sportspeople, in the next chapter.

Chapter 3

POSITIVE POWER

WHEN TALKING TO TOP ATHLETES, one characteristic that stands out is their ability to think positively – even when injured or during other tough times. The ability to see a silver lining in every cloud and turn what appears to be a negative experience into a positive helps them to succeed, time and again.

POSITIVITY COUNTS

When Sven-Göran Eriksson is selecting players for the England football team, their mental characteristics are taken into account alongside their physical skill. Whether a player has a positive outlook or not is a key issue.

'To join the team, you must have a positive attitude and you must believe that you can go to Germany and win. If they don't believe we can do it, then it's impossible; we will never win. You must have that positive attitude for everything you do in the team.

'Some mornings you wake and life is difficult; it's raining and windy, but you must have a positive attitude anyhow. If you have one or two negative players, the next morning there will be four of them. Negativity spreads like cancer.'

David Beckham is one of the England players who impresses Eriksson because of his mental strength and attitude.

'Beckham is very positive. He's still young, but he's a leader. He doesn't talk very much, but that's positive about him. He works very hard and always tries to find solutions for difficult tasks. That's important.'

In Italy, Eriksson was impressed by Roberto Mancini when he was a player, describing him as a leader too. Mancini, who went on to become manager of Lazio, has a wonderfully positive attitude and believes everything is possible. As Eriksson says, it's wonderful to work with people like that.

Jack Charlton always had a positive outlook before games, including the 1966 World Cup competition.

'I never expected us to lose. When you go onto the field, you don't go on expecting to lose. I can't remember ever going out for a game where I felt we hadn't got a chance because the other side was so good. That's truly negative thinking. I wasn't brought up that way.'

Former indoor 200m champion sprinter John Regis remained positive even when running against Michael Johnson.

'A lot of athletes would go into a race thinking, "Michael's here, I'm coming out second". I used to go into the race thinking, "Right, you put your head together and take him

out of his comfort zone – make him focus on you, and then you've got a chance to beat him." That was the game plan I had.'

BANNING NEGATIVE THINKING

Olympic gold medal-winning hurdler Sally Gunnell is a great believer in the power of the mind to influence performance. She believes that for any athlete who stands on the starting line, as much as 70% of the race outcome is shaped by mental aspects. She says that this is based on her own experiences.

'In two key races – the 1992 Olympics and 1993 World Championships – I don't think I was stronger than anybody else; I just think I was mentally prepared. I taught myself not to let any negative thoughts come in, because that's what the brain wants to do all the time. I just used to stop myself and then turn it around to say, "I can do this, I've eaten well, I've done everything I can." I fed myself loads of quality thoughts until, I guess, the brain took it all in.'

Having won the Olympic title in Barcelona in 1992, Gunnell's next major challenge was the world championships the following year. She had prepared herself mentally and was feeling good. Then a week beforehand she came down with a cold. When she arrived at the athletes' village the doctor put her on antibiotics. Suddenly something negative had entered the equation and Gunnell felt anxious about her ability to perform at her best.

'I ran the heat and felt okay. Time-wise it wasn't too bad. Then I ran the semis and felt good again. I was running a pretty reasonable time. I said to myself, "Well, if I'm going to do this, I'm going to do it properly. I can't go into the race saying to myself that I've got a cold and I've got a good excuse. I'm just going to have to go for it."

'Every single moment I would not allow this cold to get into my head. I was stopping myself coughing and feeding

*myself good thoughts. I told myself, "I'm feeling fantastic. I
can do this. I'm in the best shape ever."*

*'Every time a negative thought started I wouldn't let it
finish in my mind. I would stop it and turn it around into
something positive: "I feel really good, I've eaten fantastically well."'*

Right up to the start of the race Gunnell concentrated on not
letting her rivals realize she was slightly under the weather.
She says: 'I remember standing in the call room beforehand
and not letting everybody else know that I'd just coughed and
that I had a cold.'

When Gunnell then won the world title, and set a new world
record in the process, she was amazed:

*'I couldn't believe I'd done it. There was relief, but I was in
shock that I'd done it. I was freaked out to think that I'd
actually talked myself into doing that – into winning.'*

While some top athletes may naturally have a positive outlook
on life and on their sporting challenges, positive thinking can
be deliberately encouraged by coaches.

When former Davis Cup captain David Lloyd ran the Slater
Scheme for talented young tennis players, he worked hard to
encourage a positive attitude amongst them. His actions were
influenced by Australian tennis champion Ken Rosewall, with
whom Lloyd had lived and travelled for a period of time.

*'Ken used to say that 90% is in the mind. When I had the
Slater Scheme with kids who were 9 or 10 I tried very hard
when I did anything with them to subliminally bring up
the mind. We used to play tunes like "When the Tough Get
Going". If the kids were in the car and had had a bad day,
we'd play a tune like "One Moment in Time". I'd ask them
what they'd hear out of this song. It was all to get them
gently aware of the fact that the mind is the most important
thing. Your heart and mind win matches.'*

HARD TIMES

Few sporting careers run without a hitch. However, bad experiences can bring unexpected benefits. Professor Graham Jones believes that the elite performers who have encountered some adversity along the way can emerge even stronger champions than people who have sailed through to the top. He believes that failure can do people good as long as they can cope with it and come back from it. He has noted that many of the people who become the world's best have not had complete success along the way. On the other hand, those who have always been successful don't necessarily last for long at the top. For some reason they appear less able to handle the number one spot.

Mark Richardson the 400m runner has certainly faced adversity – and he believes he has emerged the stronger for it. Richardson suffered one of the worst things that can happen to a top athlete – being excluded from competition for using the banned substance nandralone in February 2000. He spent much of the two years following the ban arguing his innocence and trying to prove he was a victim of circumstance. Even so, he sees a positive side to the whole drama.

'I believe you are shaped by your experiences, and this whole situation has only made me mentally stronger. I believe I'm now much stronger on the track.

'It was a very difficult situation. It felt like staring down the barrel of a gun – it was completely out of my control. But during that time I continued to train and refused to give up. I drew on my own inner strength, driven by the fact I knew I hadn't done anything wrong. And part of it was just pure bloody-mindedness.'

Sir Chay Blyth also has an impressively positive outlook. He doesn't let a negative situation put him off. Instead, he always tries to turn it into a positive one.

'If I hear really bad news ... Say I'm waiting for a yacht sponsor to say "yes" and I get the message "no". I still go

*and open my bottle of champagne. It's not going to stop me.
One door closes, another one opens.'*

Injuries provide some of the toughest yet most common challenges for athletes and top sportspeople. At such times the
true champions draw deeply on their positive attitudes to
enable themselves to return to competition quickly.

Former badminton champion Gill Clark suffered from
injury problems at certain key points in her career. She recalls
how she remained positive when recovering from injury in the
run up to the European Championships.

> *'I can remember lying in my hospital bed the day after my
> first knee operation. I was stuck in plaster the physio came
> along and said, "I can't let you out of bed, not for any
> reason, until you can do ten straight leg raises." She said
> it would take me two or three days to do that. I held on to
> the bar of the bed that stopped me falling out and did ten
> straight leg raises.*
>
> *'From that moment, the day after the operation, it never
> occurred to me that I wouldn't get back into competition. I
> lay in the hospital bed and I imagined standing on the top
> of the rostrum at the European Championships, with that
> gold medal around my neck again. I'd get all excited about
> it. And therefore my training watch would go off every hour
> on the hour and I'd do ten more straight leg raises, ten min-
> utes of exercise every hour on the hour.'*

Champion 400m runner Roger Black's career was dogged
by injury, not counting a congenital heart valve problem, for
which he is monitored every year. He broke his foot in 1998
and also suffered from viral infections. Nevertheless, he is able
to put these experiences in a positive light.

Black feels that without the illnesses and injuries he might
have run faster, but he wouldn't have won his Olympic medal.
He says:

'The only reason I won Olympic silver in 1996 was because of all the things that had happened to me in the eight years prior to that. The injuries give you a burning desire, because you appreciate health so much more when you have been injured. And in 1996 I was healthy. When you have full health going into the Olympics you appreciate it so much more. I don't think I would have lasted in the sport until I was 32 if I had been healthy all the time. Your successes in life are what people see, but it's your failures and disappointments that shape you, and how you deal with those. The strength I have is not from having gold medals around my neck, but from being out of the sport for two years.'

England rugby captain Lawrence Dallaglio is a naturally confident sportsman. On match day he becomes excited at the prospect of showing what he can do, believing he's a great player. Although this isn't quite so easy when nursing an injury, Dallaglio keeps himself thinking positively.

'In an ideal world you should be 100% fit and you shouldn't really play if you are carrying an injury, but there are inevitably going to be knocks and bumps. Say you haven't had the benefit of two or three days' practice, but still get picked because it's felt you can perform. That's when you lean back on the experience of previous successes, where you haven't had an injury. You say: "I'm going to focus and concentrate on doing certain things well, that I know I'm going to do well." That helps to overcome the injury aspect.'

Positive thinking also sees the pain that comes with supreme effort as a positive and welcome thing. Professor Graham Jones has been studying the differences between the top sporting performers in the world – people who win medals in the Olympics – and international athletes who might make it to the top ten in the Olympics. He has found there are differences between even these groups. One concerns the reaction to pain. Professor Jones says that international performers who are extremely good at what they do – but not the best in the world – talk about pain and tolerating pain – coming through it. In contrast, the world's best performers also talk about pain, but they talk about loving it. They know the pain is going to happen and when it does, it's fantastic. They think: 'This is what I live for, this is what I train for, and it's great; it's here and I'm going to beat it.' As Professor Jones says, the world's top performers live for these moments; those who don't quite make it are the ones who, when they feel the pain, realize they don't really want it.

Former 400m champion Roger Black agrees that training for the 400m was not fun. It never could be because you have to push yourself so hard. Those who do well at the distance have incredible ability to thrive on the pain.

> *'Most people will not try the 400m because it hurts. Certainly with the training, you know you will suffer. Lactic acid is created more in the 400m than any other event. Psychologically, to do something five or six times a week knowing that you can't walk at the end and it will take you two hours to recover and you are going to be sick – that frightens quite a few people off. You have to have a warped sense of perspective.'*

COURAGE TO FAIL

A champion's positive outlook also demonstrates itself in the form of courage – having the courage to fail. Sportspeople who think positively accept that whenever you aim high you risk falling short, but that doesn't stop them trying or inhibit their attempt.

Having the courage to fail is essential if anyone is to make it to the top in sport; every time a champion competes there are new rivals making a challenge. Like love and hate, success and failure are extremely close bedfellows. Ron Dennis of McLaren believes that having the courage to fail isn't only essential for sports stars and racing drivers; it's vital for anyone in any activity if they are really to get the most out of life.

> *'How often do you go through life avoiding decisions because you can't contemplate the potential of failure? Lots of people don't get married because of it. Lots of people carry lots of insecurities. It holds them back in their lives.'*

Former national athletics coach Frank Dick believes there are four fears that can seriously impede a sportsperson. These are fear of losing, fear of making a mistake, fear of rejection and fear of embarrassment. Fear of losing is like thinking about drowning when you should be thinking about swimming. Worrying about making mistakes means you don't take risks, and that means no progress. Fear of rejection, in terms of not being selected, again leads to playing safe, as does fear of embarrassment or being concerned about what other people think. Dick calls these 'fatal fears' because they take people back off the edge. Champions have to want to live on the edge; they have got to be comfortable being there.

In 1993 Roger Black's running career was looking extremely uncertain and he went to Australia in order, he says, 'to escape'. He was crippled by the fear of failure.

> *'My career seemed to be nearly over, and as a person I was all over the place. Everything was a struggle. I picked up a simple book and it had a graph in it showing need for achievement and fear of failure. I looked at it and thought, "That's me. I'm scared of failure."'*

Black's fear of failure was starting to limit his performances and he decided to address this fear. He thought about what was the worst that could happen. He thought about what 'failure' meant. He realized that there was no such thing.

> *'I could lose all my money. I could lose my house. But I can't fail, because there's no such thing as failure. If you're an athlete or whatever you do, the worst thing is to be afraid of failure.'*

Black believes that you either have the ability to perform under pressure, or you don't. He suggests that Michael Jordan the basketball player lives for the moments when there are two seconds left in a game and he gets the ball. However, many players don't want that, because pressure is about the fear of failure. Black says he spent much of his career thinking about what would happen if he didn't succeed. He finally worked out that there was no such thing as failure, and when he knew that, he really had the ability to perform under pressure.

> *'When I went to the Olympic Games, I knew I couldn't fail, I knew I couldn't run a bad race. For me it was a pressure situation. There were 85,000 people in the stadium, millions of people back in Britain and a billion people round the world. It was pressure, but you don't think about those things.'*

A positive approach to life – the ability to consider experiences in a positive way – helps champions to keep going through the hard times they inevitably face when pursuing their dreams. This is the final personal characteristic we examine in Part I. In the next few pages, we draw together our key findings and suggests how we can all learn from these champions in our own lives.

Analysis I

PERSONALITY POWER

IN PART I WE FOCUSED ON personality traits of proven sporting champions, looking for common threads and sources of inspiration that helped to make them successful over and over again when competing at the highest level.

CHAPTER 1

In Chapter 1: True Grit, we found that champions often show a natural sense of discipline, being able to train regularly and effectively, often from an early age.

They recognize that if they are to achieve their best possible performance in the heat of competition, then they have to make choices – sometimes tough choices – about how they spend their time. They can't live a 'normal' life like the rest of us, but must be prepared to train when others are asleep; or to put their social and personal lives second to their sporting activities.

Champions show great determination – what Ron Dennis, boss of the McLaren racing team, calls 'steely resolve'. The need for discipline and determination may mean that champions have to be selfish if they are to achieve their ambitions. They have to focus their time and energies on themselves.

Renzie Hanham from mental conditioning specialists Gazing Performance notes that elite performers have the ability to *accept* conditions of extreme discomfort, both physical and psychological, and to carry on functioning. Hanham explains that acceptance doesn't mean you have to like what's happening or that you agree or acquiesce. What it does mean is that you accept the present moment for what it is. This is important because when you accept, you cease resisting and thus free up your attention to seek solutions to the challenges you face.

Hanham notes that elite performers develop this ability over time by repeatedly putting themselves 'at risk' and developing coping mechanisms for dealing with high-pressure situations. In addition to their physical training and skills development, they undertake deliberate mental conditioning – training their minds to be able to remain focused on the processes they need to complete in order to be successful. In this way they develop the resilience they will need to win gold medals and claim world championships.

Repeated winners also have a strong 'killer instinct'. They won't feel sympathy for the opponent they are about to defeat; they won't quaver at the thought that they just need one more point to win Wimbledon. They seize their chances with relish. As far as javelin champion Steve Backley is concerned, he is a warrior doing battle and fighting for his life.

Not everyone has this killer instinct to the same degree. If you don't really mind whether you come in the top three or not, let alone come first, then you probably won't be a champion. The same goes in other areas of life too. If you don't mind whether you are an accounts clerk or a financial director, then you are more likely to remain as a clerk, because becoming a financial director requires years of training, hard work and pressure.

None of the personal characteristics we found in the champions we interviewed can compensate for a lack of physical talent and training. Similarly, there is no doubt that you can't expect to be a consistent winner in any area of life outside sport without having the fundamental talent and competence required for that activity. If you have the essential ability required for what you want to do, you then need to build up the skill levels required bit by bit. That also means that, unless you are uniquely gifted, you will need a high degree of determination and discipline to succeed. As the saying goes, Rome wasn't built in a day.

Applications

- Recall times in your life when you showed some discipline or determination. These may be in any area – completing a difficult school project, working late to prepare a presentation or training to complete a long-distance charity walk. Understand that you have the ability to display these characteristics when you are motivated to do so.
- What are you trying to achieve now? Confirm to yourself that you have the commitment required. If you have doubts, consider whether you are sufficiently motivated: do you really want to train for a new job?

CHAPTER 2

In Chapter 2: I Believe!, we focused on the depth and strength of the champions' self-belief. Time and again, champions demonstrate a virtually unshakeable self-belief in their abilities.

The key question is, can that degree of self-belief be developed or is it innate? For many of our champions, their self-belief developed over time as they began winning competitions. As they moved up through to the higher levels of their sports and kept on winning, that self-belief became stronger. It certainly didn't appear overnight. David Platt, former England football captain, only began to think 'I can do this' when he had scored goals repeatedly in international matches.

Ceri Evans from mental conditioning specialists Gazing Performance explains that, for sustained sporting success to occur, self-belief has to be underpinned by competence, which means that developing self-belief is an incremental process. Self-belief is likely to have stronger foundations if confidence is gained in tandem with competence. It is vulnerable unless those skills have been tested in situations of increasing pressure.

Some top champions describe the self-belief they have as a sense of 'knowing' they will do well. However, that belief often results from a period of consistent training and peak performances, when the individual is in top shape and injury free. It also comes from knowing that they have trained hard and are perfectly prepared. For Sally Gunnell, for example, self-belief came from knowing she had done all she could in the run-up to the competition, from training well to eating a healthy diet.

Champions don't limit themselves by limiting their beliefs or expectations. The self-fulfilling prophecy applies to sporting champions as it does to anyone else. They learn that how they perceive a competitor can influence their own performance. As sprinter John Regis found out, if you put someone on a pedestal, it becomes impossible to knock them off. If he allowed himself to be intimidated by the reputations of Frankie Fredericks, Michael Johnson and Linford Christie, he pushed himself into a losing position before a race even started.

The ability to bounce back is a trait that many of our champions display. When they are injured and prevented from training or competing, they still somehow hold onto the belief that they will come back and win again. Even if they have suffered an unexpected loss or a period of disappointing performances, they still have the ability to raise their game once more and become a winner again.

Applications

- Think back to times in your life when you felt confident about something you were doing or were about to do, and that went well. Try to identify why you were feeling confident. Had you prepared for it in some way? Had you done a similar activity before? Had someone advised you about or encouraged you in the activity?
- Think about something you want to do or will have to do in future, that you don't currently feel confident about. Can you apply anything from the exercise above to this activity? Is there anything you could do to prepare, that would develop your skills and so improve your self-confidence? Is there anyone with experience in this area who could advise you?
- Try to identify any areas of your life where the self-limiting prophecy applies. This could be at home, at work or in any area of your life. If you are a golfer, do you tell yourself you're no good at bunker shots and so always make a tough situation even harder when you find yourself in the sand? Make a promise to yourself that you will challenge these self-limiting beliefs wherever you spot them. Try asking yourself how you could improve your performance in the area, rather than just judging yourself poorly.

CHAPTER 3

The ability to focus on the positive aspects of an experience, rather than the negative ones, is a trait that many champions show, and one we considered in Chapter 3: Positive Power. Sven-Göran Eriksson considers whether a player has a positive outlook, as well as his football talent, when selecting members of the England squad.

Being able to feel positive and avoid negative thoughts was important to hurdler Sally Gunnell when she was competing for her Olympic and world championship medals.

Developing this kind of outlook can be helped over time, by coaches encouraging young sportspeople to learn from their experiences – whether good or bad.

In fact, facing setbacks early in a sporting career can make the emerging champions stronger and tougher later on. If they have overcome a challenging situation before, or come back from injury in the past, that experience gives them added belief that they can do so again.

Top champions can even see pain in a positive light. They are able to tolerate pain and extreme discomfort, in training and in competition, because they see it as bringing them the sporting success they desire. The same approach can be applied in ordinary, non-sporting life. You may not be looking forward to completing a certain piece of work, but once you have done it and done it well, maybe you will be one step nearer promotion.

For some champions, their success results from not being afraid to fail. They accept that if they aim high, they increase the risk of failure, but that doesn't stop them from trying.

Clearly our sporting champions have high levels of skill and competence underpinning their positive outlooks. Renzie Hanham from mental conditioning specialists Gazing Performance notes the importance of positive thinking being supported by reality in the form of competence. He says that too often, in many areas of life, people mistake confidence for competence. If you just think you can do something but never initiate an action plan of how to develop the necessary skills, you will never be able to function optimally at the highest level.

Applying a positive outlook to life is a skill that can be developed. We can be moody, negative and depressed if we choose to be so, but by focusing on processes rather than our emotions we can learn to create positive outcomes from the situations and experiences we encounter.

However, it is not enough to simply tell someone to think positively. As Ceri Evans from Gazing Performance explains, if you do that, you may just add to the busy and conflicted dialogue going on in that person's head. It is usually more effective to encourage people to focus attention on the processes that lead to their desired outcomes, rather than the outcomes themselves. In other words, if you are feeling negative about a piece of work, trying to convince yourself that things will work out positively may be counter-productive. It is often more useful to return your focus of attention to what you need to do to complete the work effectively. Once you start focusing on these processes, emotional responses can move into the background and become less distracting.

Applications

- Try to get in the habit of thinking about the processes involved in the things you do, rather than your emotional responses to them. For example, rather than fuming about the fact that you have five more tasks to complete before you can go home for the weekend, focus on what you need to do to complete them quickly and effectively.
- What is it that you are feeling negative about? Look for anything positive that is associated with it. For example, if you are feeling negative about having to study for a professional exam, remind yourself that you are aiming to gain a qualification that will better your career in the long term.

Part II

MOTIVATIONAL MATTERS

Chapter 4

THE SUCCESS MAGNET

STRONG MOTIVATION IS AN ABSOLUTELY ESSENTIAL requirement for any sporting champion. The dedication required to train constantly, push the body to the limits and cope with competitive pressure can only be sustained where there are strong drivers to succeed.

Steve Sylvester, sports psychologist, says that world champions have an ability to sacrifice to the extreme, but where does that come from? Is it because it's a dream planted in them over the years? Or is it because there's a deep-seated need that they have to satisfy?

In research conducted by Professor Graham Jones, motivation emerges as a key requirement for joining the sporting elite. The champion sportspeople Professor Jones involved in his research determined that the fourth most important characteristic of mental toughness was: 'Having an insatiable desire and internalized motives to succeed'.

Former double Olympic 1500m champion Sebastian Coe has read widely on the topic of what it is that makes a champion sportsperson, but he has developed his own view of what really makes the difference between a champion's drive and the rest.

> *'Everybody is different; we're all motivated by very different things, for extrinsic reasons and intrinsic reasons. Some people want to be successful because they like the idea of having a big house and a Porsche on the drive; others want to do it to explore how hard and how mentally tough they are.*
>
> *'For most of us it's probably a mixture of all those things. If you ask me, the one continuum that runs through all those different models is just, actually, the bloody-minded self-determination to be better than the next person.'*

NEEDING TO WIN

For many champions, the need to be first – to win – exceeds everything else. Coming second just isn't good enough.

World-beating 1500m champion Sebastian Coe relished the big occasions. He learnt early on that what mattered was winning major titles, and that was what he set his heart on. Coe says he loved running and he enjoyed training, but the real thing that excited him was competing in major championships. He says he always knew the difference between going into a year where there were big races but no major championships, and going into a year where he knew that in August he was going to defend an Olympic title or hope to win a European title. Coe says:

> *'When I was 18 I was racing up at Gateshead. The night before one of the races I had supper with Brendan Foster, who was a big influence on me. Brendan always said to me that at the end of your career, if you put your cards down*

*on the table to declare, people would ask what medals you
had won. They wouldn't ask whether you had won Zurich
in 1978. It would be, how many Olympic titles did you win?
How many world records did you break? Brendan made me
realize that major championships were important and the
other races, as important as they were, were only building
blocks along the way. They weren't the be-all and end-all.'*

For round-the-world yachtswoman Ellen MacArthur, winning
is key when she's sailing competitively. That doesn't mean it's
the only thing she thinks about when she's out at sea, because
the lengths of races vary so much. Sometimes just completing
the race is an achievement. As she says, in a round-the-world
race it's a miracle just to get round without stopping. What
makes sailing in a race so hard is that you are pushing so hard.
Then MacArthur says, there's never a second of any day when
you're not thinking about whether you're sailing the boat to its
full potential.

When MacArthur was preparing to compete in *Kingfisher*
in the Vendée Globe, her goals were high.

*'My objective was to get across that line first. I knew in real-
ity that some of the other guys had a lot more experience
and stood a good chance of winning the race. There were
several boats that I believed at the start could have won the
Vendée Globe. But your objective is to do well and never
give up. If you think, "Oh well, I'm just going to finish third
anyway," you may as well stop. You'd probably end up being
fifth or sixth. You have to keep driving; it's not over until you
get to that finish line.'*

England 1966 World Cup footballer Jack Charlton admits that
he was never a particularly good player – but he had a winning
attitude.

*'I had a good head into the ball, and I was pretty hard to run
away from. I was never quick off the mark, but I had a little*

mean streak in me – and that's the need to win. You want to win. You've got to have that need to win.'

EARLY TASTE OF SUCCESS

Adrian Moorhouse, Olympic swimming champion, found that his ability in the pool gave him an early liking for the sweet taste of success. Doing well at sport became linked with his sense of self-esteem. Winning felt good.

Moorhouse describes himself as having been quite a small, shy child. However, he was a good swimmer, competing in local competitions as a member of Bradford Swimming Club, and success in the pool was important for his sense of self-esteem.

'When I was 12, in 1976, David Wilkie won the Olympics. As a kid I didn't have much going for me. I didn't have many mates. I was pretty small and very shy, so I latched onto something that made me feel good about myself. I was the sort of kid who would run back from school down the road imagining I was a great athlete, winning the Olympics. I was always imagining myself being good and being applauded. A lot of it is to do with self-esteem.'

Moorhouse vividly remembers winning his first swimming medal, and it's a moment he still treasures.

'I still have the little medal. I keep it in the same box as my Olympic gold medal. I won this first gold when I was nine, for the nine-and-under backstroke in the Airdale Championships at Harrogate. I remember the pool and everything about it. My arms were going round like windmills to get there first and I hit my hand on the end of the pool. I remember walking back down the side – it was only one length – to collect my tracksuit. I remember feeling really proud – inflated with pride – and looking at my mum and dad. It was a big night.'

OVERWHELMING EMOTIONS

Former badminton champion Gill Clark found winning a fantastic feeling. The sheer joy she has experienced through her sport, and all the emotions that have come from it, have surpassed anything else on a happy level. The highs of winning are higher, but the lows are nowhere near as low, she says. The disappointment that comes from failing to achieve a desired result in a major championship is nothing in comparison to the hurt that people can feel in their private lives – for example, the pain she felt when her father became ill.

When Clark became an international player and began to realize her talent, winning was a personal affair. She was proud to represent her nation, but that wasn't her main motivation for doing well.

> *'I was hugely honoured to play for my country. When you are at the Commonwealth Games and competing for England, or in the Olympics for Great Britain, that gives you an extra pride. But you don't go out and perform for your country – you go out and perform for you, solely for you.'*

Former Davis Cup tennis captain, David Lloyd, loved winning. He says:

> *'It meant a lot. If you're going to be successful in life, winning is your food. Winning is your payment. I played Davis Cup for nine or ten years. I didn't lose at home. You can't take that away. And we beat guys who were Wimbledon champions.'*

For champion hurdler Sally Gunnell, the realization that she had won Olympic gold in Barcelona took a while to sink in. Those first moments after winning were moments of disbelief rather than exhilaration.

> *'I had gone through this race so much in my mind that I felt I could well have been lying on a bed visualizing it. So*

I didn't know whether this was actually the real race. I was thinking, "Is this for real?" It feels like you're in a cocoon. It's like it's all in slow motion. Then you start to realize what's happened.

'One of my friends came running onto the track and you start jogging around. I did my lap of honour and started spotting people in the crowd. I saw Linford Christie up there shouting his head off at me. I remember hearing my dad's voice in the crowd and seeing his face – amidst all the thousands of people there. That's when I first thought this was going to make a big difference to my life. Then I saw my husband Jon and it started to sink in. But it was still so weird and I had a sense of disbelief that I'd done it.'

The feeling of achievement, once there, was powerful. Gunnell says:

'You are just floating. You are on a cloud. I've never taken drugs, but you just don't feel as though you're there. I used to say I wanted to find a little box and be able to put it all inside and just go away. Then six months later I'd open it up and see it all again. I just couldn't take it all in at the time.'

Former European 200m champion sprinter John Regis just wanted to be the best in the world. Making it to a final and knowing he was among the top eight in the world wasn't enough. He didn't want to be top eight; he wanted to be the top person in the world.

In 1990 Regis won a bronze in the 100m in the European Championships in Split. He then took gold in the 200m.

'When I won I thought, "Yeah, this is why I train hard, this is why it's all worthwhile." Athletics is hard. In winter it's cold and nasty. You vomit for three and a half months of the year. Your legs are full of lactic acid. But I'll take twenty minutes of pain a day in return for standing on that rostrum. No problem at all.

'It's like having a dream, going to heaven and waking up and you're sitting on top of the world. You go to the rostrum and the announcer is saying, "In first place, John Regis". You stand up there and look at the crowd cheering. You think "Wow!" All the work I had done, all the pain I had gone through flashed through my mind in the blink of an eye. It's like climbing Everest. Everyone is congratulating you.'

Champion National Hunt jockey Richard Dunwoody managed to win the Grand National twice, first with West Tip in 1986. He tried to savour the feeling second time round when he won in 1994.

'For my second Grand National win I rode Freddie Starr's horse, Miinnehoma. I didn't expect to get round. It rained very heavily and we knew that probably only five or six horses would complete the course. I'd only ridden Miinnehoma once before in a race and schooled him once at home. He wasn't big. I thought he'd end up on the floor and I was quite expecting to be getting an ambulance rather than having Martin Pipe, the trainer, run up to me at the end of the race. So that was by far the most memorable race. The first time you win the National it's a complete blur – you don't come down out of cloud nine for three or four days afterwards. With the second win, I spent a lot of time taking it in and actually enjoying the success.'

When Dunwoody began to experience success, he just wanted more. He was driven to win.

'Success brings success. Success drove you on to more success. You got on that wagon and you just couldn't get off it. It became totally all consuming. There were about three seasons where I finished second in the championship. The one aim then was to become champion jockey.'

BEATING YOURSELF

For some top sportspeople, the motivation isn't just to beat others but also to amaze themselves by their own achievements.

England rugby fly-half Jonny Wilkinson derives immense satisfaction from kicking a goal that wins the game or provides enough of a buffer to really put pressure on the opposition. He says he sometimes amazes himself when he pulls off a difficult kick.

'For me personally it comes down to constantly trying to impress myself. I may be kicking the ball from right out on the touchline and there's a breeze across the posts. The margin for error is very small. I have to aim exactly just inside the left-hand post, because the wind should push it across slightly so that it goes through the middle.

'You do all your preparation and hit the ball. Everything feels right and you look up and see that it's exactly just inside the left-hand post. The wind does move it that little bit and it does go through the middle. Most of the time you find yourself thinking, "Crikey" rather than "That's just what I do". You need a balance of setting high standards and trying to achieve them, and then also being able to pat yourself on the back when there was a real need to get it perfect and you got it right.'

Round-the-world yachtswoman Ellen MacArthur is also motivated by the desire to keep challenging herself. She set herself tough challenges from an early age. She believes one of her greatest challenges was to sail a 20-foot boat single-handed round the coast of Great Britain when she was 18.

'That still fills me with amazement. You could say it was the toughest race ever to date, but every race you do pushes you to your limits and that's how you learn. When I sailed round Britain in a little 20-footer, I was pushing myself to

my absolute limits to make it. It was a tiny boat and a really hard trip to do. It took me four and a half months.

'Then the next thing I did was a single-handed transatlantic race. Alright, I sailed twice across the Atlantic in bigger boats first as a test, but then I crossed the Atlantic on my own in a race and that again was a massive test. It was the hardest thing I'd ever done.'

After that, completing the Vendée Globe became the next hardest challenge for MacArthur.

'I pushed myself further in the Vendée than in any race before, but I know that in future I'm going to take myself to those same limits. Life's about pushing yourself further and learning and that's what I intend to do.'

Ron Roddan, who worked with Linford Christie throughout his competitive career and who has coached many athletes over the years, certainly believes that champions are always striving for improvement.

'After any major race, athletes would come back and ask, "What did you think?" Well, you should never have a perfect race. If you have a perfect race, where do you go? You may as well finish. For a champion, perfection is always around the next corner. You are never satisfied.'

Similarly, former England football Under-21 manager David Platt believes really great players are always striving to be better than they are. He says:

'When Michael Owen was earning £10,000 a week he didn't want £20,000 a week – he wanted to be a better player. I don't know what Michael is earning now, but whatever it is, he doesn't want more money – he wants to be a better player. And if he gets more money his edge doesn't go down, his performance level doesn't go down. Michael just wants to do better.'

Platt recalls Owen's determination to be the best when he was at the School of Excellence as an early teenager.

'There was a speed test. You set off and ran through to the other end, turned round and came back. It was a speed and power test, because you had to turn. We sat them all down afterwards and told them their times. Michael wasn't the fastest, but he said there was no way he hadn't got the quickest time in. He made us let him do it again. He just wouldn't accept that he wasn't fastest. He's unbelievable. That's being a winner.'

The need to win, and the thrill that comes from achieving goals, is clearly a powerful motivator for many top sportspeople. In the next chapter we consider how the desire not to fail also drives many champions forward.

Chapter 5

FLEEING FAILURE

THE FACTORS THAT MOTIVATE PEOPLE – whether sportspeople or anyone else – can usually be divided into two camps. Firstly, there are motivating factors that attract people – the thrill of winning, the elation that can come with achievement, as considered in the previous chapter.

On the other hand, there are also powerful 'away from' motivators. Some people may hate to lose so badly that they push themselves harder than anyone else. Some people are frightened of letting other people down, a fear that drives them to even greater efforts to win.

HATING TO LOSE

Ron Dennis, boss of the McLaren racing team, doesn't just 'need' to win. He hates the pain of failure.

'The gratification of success is easily matched by the pain of failure. Whilst you would initially think that the biggest driver is the search for the rush of success, it doesn't drive you as much as the pain of failure. I feel psychological pain in failure, and it's a great motivator.'

That said, for Dennis it's important to feel you have won well. He says the worst feeling for him, even if he is winning, is to think that he didn't give something his best shot. In contrast he can get satisfaction from coming second if he knows he gave it everything. The frustration of not winning is there, but it is softened by the sense that there was nothing more that could have been done.

Former England rugby head coach Clive Woodward believes that fear of losing helps to motivate the England team.

'The biggest thing, especially with the Six Nations, is that you've got to create a fear factor – a respect factor. In some games it's not difficult; if we are playing a team we can clearly lose to, the fear factor is there. The difficult games are against teams we know we can lose to, but we know we really should beat – so you've got to create this fear factor. This England team certainly plays far better when there's this real fear factor. That's why we tend to play better against the bigger teams – we tend to play better when there's some-thing at stake. We knew that if we wanted to do something special in the World Cup, we would have to beat these big teams week in, week out. You've got to be meticulous in the detail and the easier the opposition, the more meticulous you've got to be.'

Champion 400m runner Roger Black isn't clear where his motivation to succeed in athletics came from, but he feels he was driven strongly by the desire to move away from the pain of failure. That had a greater motivating force on him than the pleasure of success.

'If you work on the pain and pleasure principle, you have to go away from pain or towards pleasure. The great pain to me in life is to look back and know that I didn't do something properly – whatever it is. For me it's about being able to say I did as well as I wanted to, or as well as I could.'

Round-the-world yachtswoman Ellen MacArthur's sense of all the people who have worked behind the scenes to get her racing across the ocean helps her to give her all when the going gets really tough. For example, when competing in the Vendeé Globe she had to climb up a mast to make emergency repairs.

'With a project like the Vendeé I'm not just doing it for me. A huge amount of energy and commitment goes into preparing for a race like that. There are so many people who prepared the boat and then who are working every day, communicating with you. There's all that energy behind you and it's not up to you to give in. You're damn well going to hang on in there and not let anyone down. Probably fear of failure is one of the biggest motivators – not wanting to let people down.'

PROVING OTHERS WRONG

A different form of 'away from' motivator is the desire not to give others the satisfaction of being right when they have told you that you can't do something. For some champions, this desire to prove others wrong has provided a major spur to achievement.

Olympic hurdle gold medallist Sally Gunnell recalls how many people said she would never win because she was not 'hard enough'. Comments like that spurred her on to try harder. Gunnell recalls one such spur.

*'There was a guy at the top of athletics organizing Grand
Prix and so on. He actually said to me that I would never
make it, because I was the wrong colour, the wrong size. He
said I wasn't in the glory events – I wasn't a sprinter. He stood
there as a 45-year-old man telling me, a 17-year-old, that I
may as well forget it, that I would never be good enough. He
wouldn't give me the break that I wanted – he wouldn't give
me the races that I wanted to try and progress.*

*'Part of me thought that maybe he was right and I should
try and find another career and give up on athletics. But
luckily, deep down I thought, "No. So what if I'm not black
and I'm not six foot tall and I haven't got the longest legs in
the business?" I decided I was going to prove him wrong.
It was one of the first setbacks that really made me think,
"Yes, I can do this." This was the first time I started setting
myself goals, including that dream goal of being Olympic
champion.'*

Like Gunnell, middle distance runner Sebastian Coe recalls
being told that he didn't have what it would take to excel at his
chosen sport. He also proved his detractors wrong. Coe says:

*'I was told when I was 18 that I was too small, not tall
enough, to be a good 800m runner. I rather enjoyed proving them wrong there. I was also told I would never make
a 1500m runner and I rather enjoyed proving them wrong
too.'*

Former Davis Cup tennis captain David Lloyd, now a successful businessman, still enjoys proving others wrong.

*'I've had more success in business in sport, and I think one
of the reasons I get a real kick out of it is because I was told
so many times that I was a dumb idiot: "You're a tennis
player – you can't do it". A lot of people do things because
other people say they can't. I'm sure Steve Redgrave won
another gold medal because people said it was impossible*

to do. Anything that's impossible is worth going for. When people say "you can't", I think, "Right, I'm going to do it".'

THE RELIEF OF SUCCESS

The fact that champions are driven by not wanting to experience the pain of failure is indicated by the sense of relief many feel when they succeed. For them the winning sensation isn't all euphoria and high emotions.

Michael Lynagh, the former Australian rugby captain, is one of Rugby Union's modern greats and Australia's greatest ever fly-half. He scored 911 points in 72 appearances for his country – until recently, the highest number of points scored in international rugby. Lynagh had a strong competitive streak regardless of what sport he was playing. His desire to achieve and do as well as he could was very strong. At one stage he couldn't play any sport, whether golf, tennis or anything else, without treating it extremely competitively – to an extent that was almost embarrassing. He has mellowed with time, however. He says he can now play sport and be pretty relaxed about it. He realizes that the result doesn't really matter and so he can just go out and enjoy it a bit more. That sense of perspective developed towards the end of his career in rugby. He began to see sports other than rugby as providing a form of stress release.

Winning didn't necessarily deliver a great buzz, however. Lynagh's greatest win was perhaps the World Cup in 1991 at Twickenham.

'I knew it was a huge occasion, but I can't remember much of the game. You go into a daze where you are just doing what you do. When we won, I felt triumph, satisfaction and relief. Fantastic though it was, my overwhelming feeling was a sense of relief that the opportunity had come and I had taken it. I find it difficult to get too excited about it. I guess I would get more emotional about it if we had lost.'

Lynagh also found it difficult to talk about his successes.

> *'I thought modesty was very important. Accept what you have got, and be thankful for it. If you are successful at things – that's very nice, thank you, but I don't want to talk about it.'*

Professor Graham Jones has confirmed through his research that achieving major success doesn't always generate as euphoric a feeling as might be expected. For one thing, there is often a substantial amount of relief mixed in with the euphoria. That can come from the realization that other people have high expectations of your performance. Professor Jones gives the example of Steve Redgrave when gearing up for the Sydney Olympics. Everyone expected him to do well and would have been disappointed if he hadn't. Winning in such circumstances must inevitably be associated with feelings of relief as much as jubilation.

Secondly, some people feel a sense of anticlimax, because of the extent of all the build-up and preparation beforehand. When they achieve their goal they sometimes expect to feel more than they do, particularly if the achievement is one that the individual has been striving towards over a long period of time. Finally, given the packed sporting timetables that many champions face, they may not have much time to celebrate their successes before gearing up for the next competition. That means they simply have to control their euphoria and quickly get back to the business of training and preparation.

Winning – whether it brings euphoria or relief – always marks the achievement of a sporting goal. We look at the importance of goals and goal-setting for champions in the next chapter.

Chapter 6

GOALS GALORE

EVERY CHAMPION ATHLETE, FOOTBALLER AND SWIMMER – every top sportsperson – sets goals. Without goals, no one fulfils a dream to be the best, to win Olympic gold or to set a new world record.

Champion 400m runner Roger Black believes that it is absolutely essential for champions to set goals. He says that if you set a goal, then your subconscious will attract things that will support that goal. If you don't set a goal, you'll drift. Black has no doubt about this. He also points out that goal-setting is an important activity, because if you make your goals too hard, you'll destroy yourself; if you make them too easy you're going to underperform.

Sir Chay Blyth has always been goal-oriented and derives huge satisfaction from fulfilling his goals.

'With any project I take a blank sheet of paper and I write down the aim of the exercise – the goal – and take it from there. It's very fulfilling when you've written down an aim, planned everything and then you bring it to a successful conclusion. It's tremendous. I use the same process for business that I used for my sailing adventures. I set down the goals, I set down all the relevant factors involved and carry on from there.'

Olympic hurdle gold medallist Sally Gunnell also believes that goal-setting is invaluable, as long as the targets are reasonable.

'Even from a young age it's great to set your goals. But it's important to have your dream goal and realistic ones. Too many athletes have a dream goal and haven't worked out how they are going to get there. Then they just get disappointment after disappointment and never build up confidence.

'You need realistic goals that are achievable – whether it's getting into the club team or jumping a certain distance. Make them achievable.'

Goals also need to be fired with passion, linked to the individual's emotions to inspire them. Sports psychologist Ian Lynagh says that goals provide direction, while desire gives energy and passion. If coaches can help athletes develop an emotional attachment to their goals, then they are energizing and empowering the athlete to achieve them. He says a goal that is just cerebral, without any energy or emotional empowerment, is usually not achieved. It is, however, if someone feels strongly about it.

Effective goal-setting requires real commitment, which can be demonstrated by writing the goals down – committing them to paper. Former Davis Cup captain David Lloyd did this in his competitive playing days.

'I would write my goals down. If I had Wimbledon coming up a goal might be to get to the last 16, and I would write

down what I wanted to do. Next year I want to be number 7, then the year after something else. I had achievement goals and improvement goals – such as to work on my backhand.'

GOAL TYPES

The goals that athletes use aren't simply related to winning a title. There are different types of goal that all play an important part in the competitive athlete's training.

As Professor Graham Jones explains, there are three types of goals that sports psychologists talk about and sportsmen and women typically use. Firstly, there is the outcome goal – the aim being simply to win. That, however, is dependent on how people perform, so they also need to have performance goals, such as swimming the race in 60 seconds. Thirdly there are process goals, which mean that the swimmer will swim the race in a particular style – perhaps focusing on particular aspects of technique.

Athletes will use different combinations of these goals, depending on where they are in their training programme. For example, Professor Jones says, at a certain time some athletes may not be so bothered about actually winning a race; what they are focusing on is the particular performance (such as the time) and the process (the push off from the starting blocks). Professor Jones says:

'Adrian Moorhouse talks about how he apparently failed in Los Angeles in 1984 because he came fourth in the world. He was expected to come first. He focused on outcome goals – winning – and he realized that he needed people to help him build other goals. His goals in 1988 were different. Sure, they were to win – that's what kept him motivated for four years – but the other goals were about swimming a time and swimming in a particular style. One process goal he had for the 1988 Olympics was to stay strong and hold his stroke in the last five or ten metres. In the race, he won

it in the last five metres. He won it by a fingernail. So that process goal won him his Olympic gold medal.'

Sports psychologist Ian Lynagh confirms the importance of making use of the different types of goals. He says it is important for an athlete to be able to separate goals into outcome and performance goals. The outcome goals keep the athlete motivated and give them a sense of direction, but they have to focus on performance goals. Lynagh says:

'Going out to play a game of rugby and saying your goal is to win is a bullshit goal. Of course you want to win, but what are your goals today? Maybe you want to make more tackles in the opposition's half. Good athletes always have performance goals and if they achieve them, they maximize their chances of getting an outcome goal.'

Former England rugby head coach, Clive Woodward, encourages every member of the squad to set goals. He says:

'We have individual goals in terms of certain aspects of the game. All our goals are performance related, things that are measurable even if they are subjective. We try to set the standards higher than any other team in world rugby.'

As for himself, Woodward now has one overarching goal.

'My only goal is for England to be the best team in the world. I make no apologies for that. The only reason I wake up in the morning is for England to be the number one team in the world – not just Europe.'

In addition to outcome and performance goals, process goals focus on the manner in which the sportsperson wants to perform. Dr Stephanie Cook used all types of goals when training to compete in modern pentathlon.

'I used to have a sports psychology session once a week. We covered lots of aspects, including setting your goals. Those might be in terms of results, or performance related, but also process related. For example, instead of focusing on a particular time that you wanted to achieve, you might focus on the fact that you wanted to stay relaxed during the race.'

EARLY GOALS

Top sporting performers are habitual goal-setters. Michael Lynagh, former Australian rugby captain and renowned fly-half, began setting goals for himself in his childhood. He recalls how when he was in an Under-12 school cricket team he wanted to play for the Under-13s. The Under-13s played in long white trousers on grass pitches, whereas the Under-12s played in shorts on concrete. It was a simple, but powerful, early goal.

As a professional rugby player, Lynagh's goals were, not surprisingly, more sophisticated than those he set himself as a child.

'I would think about my percentage, and how I could improve it. I would think where I was missing goals from, or whether I wasn't kicking as well from my left as my right. I had specific performance skills goals that needed to be achieved. I never set out saying, "I am going to win the World Cup", though if you'd have asked me I'd have said it would be nice.'

Javelin champion Steve Backley set his first goal soon after taking up the javelin. He tried throwing it at school and enjoyed it, even though he wasn't particularly good at first. However, he decided he wanted to throw further than one particular boy, which meant he would need to throw about 30m. So, Backley went to a local field, put a marker down and kept throwing. In this way he proved himself a natural goal-setter. He set his outcome goal (beating the boy) and broke it down into a performance target (the required distance) and then practised the throw. Only later did he discover that was the correct model for goal-setting.

The process of continually setting new goals came easily to Backley.

'It's something I did naturally. If you create a goal and achieve it, the first thing you do is create a higher goal. And when you achieve that, you create another higher goal. If you do that six times on the trot you develop a real sense of achievement. I never really saw anything beyond my immediate goal. I wasn't even confident enough to say I could be British Champion.'

Backley is still setting goals – including winning gold at the 2004 Olympics. This, he says, would be the icing on the cake. Though happy with his achievements so far, Backley says he is as keen as ever to win gold. As competitions approach, he can still develop the necessary levels of desire and the need to win. However, Backley prefers to focus on process rather than outcome goals. For example, he would rather focus on optimizing his running at the throw, rather than thinking about gold.

'I am very uncomfortable broadcasting medals. OK, it's an outcome goal, and you need that if you're lacking desire. But if you're full of desire, all you need is direction. I want to win. That's what I set my life up to do.'

Champion National Hunt jockey, Richard Dunwoody, dreamt of riding in the Grand National from an early age. Brought up near Belfast in Northern Ireland, his father trained horses and horses were in his blood from the start.

'The Grand National really captured my imagination from the age of four or five. My dream wasn't so much about being a champion jockey, but about riding in the Grand National. When I became a teenager we moved to New-

market and I wanted to be a flat jockey, but unfortunately my weight was never going to allow that.

'From the day I left school my goal was to get a ride, first in a point-to-point, then on the course, then to ride a winner, then to ride more winners. In the first season I had 4 winners; the next year I had 24. From that time on it was always to ride more winners the next year, and for about 11 or 12 seasons I did ride more winners every year. Then my final goal was to be champion jockey.'

GOAL DEVELOPMENT

Adrian Moorhouse began setting his first goals early on, as a young swimmer inspired by the success of David Wilkie in the 1976 Olympics. At the age of 14, he transferred from Bradford Swimming Club to Leeds, where he found himself an Olympic coach.

'Terry Denison was one of the Olympic team coaches in 1980 and he was the head coach at Leeds. He asked me what I wanted to do, and why I was there. That's when I said, 'I want to win the Olympics because I've seen David Wilkie do it.' Terry started talking about how it might be possible. He made me look at what I was doing, and what I needed to do. The first question he asked me was: "If you're going to win the Olympics, what time are you going to win it in?" I had no idea.'

Denison effectively broke the big dream – winning Olympic gold – into a series of staging posts, starting with winning the Yorkshire title, then the North East of England and junior England titles.

But first was Yorkshire. Moorhouse had come second the year before, but now Denison wanted him to win. After that, he wanted him to come in the top three in the North East. That aim was broken down into a time goal and a performance goal, which led to highlighting the areas of Moorhouse's technique that needed work. Moorhouse says:

'Terry was giving me the agenda and making it real. That's an important skill in life – going for something big and then working out what you can do in reality today. I'm a great believer in creating the future from the future. Don't shoot low and worry about failing; don't be easy on yourself. Be hard on yourself but know how to deal with failure. Go to win the Olympics and if you don't win, then deal with it. If you ultimately miss it by just a little bit, at least you've still done something great.

'By having milestones or benchmarks you've also got a way of measuring your progress. Lots of people want to do things – lose weight, stop smoking and so on. Okay, they are big things, so how are you going to break it down and plan for them? Don't be a dreamer, be a planner.'

Throughout his competitive swimming career Moorhouse sat down every New Year's Eve and thought about what he wanted to achieve in the coming year. He highlighted each championship and the time he wanted to achieve.

'I would do that myself and then get together with my coach. We'd start breaking the goals down. There were three phases: outcome, performance and process.'

Sally Gunnell began goal-setting from an early age, and once she met her coach, Bruce Longden, they would sit down and agree her goals together. Each year she tried to set realistic goals. Some years the goals weren't achievable, and then Gunnell says she would work out why and what went wrong. On the other hand, when she did achieve her goals, her confidence grew. Achieving her goal of winning the county championships, for example, gave her the confidence to get into junior internationals, then senior internationals and then major championships. Gunnell recalls her goals for 1986.

'The achievement for that year was to get into the Commonwealth Games team. It was probably my first major

championship. I got into the team and then went on to win it. I think that was because I was on such a high.

'In 1988, which was the year of the Seoul Olympics, my goal that year was to get into an Olympic final. I got to the final and came fifth. I came away thinking, "In four years' time I can be the Olympic champion."'

The target for 1992 was to win Olympic gold.

'We planned back from there. We knew that I was going to be at my peak on my thirteenth or fourteenth race. Bruce had worked that out for years leading up to the Olympics. So we would plan every single race and Bruce would know every single training session. Having been my coach for so long he'd worked out what my body needed. He knew how every individual was different. He knew what sessions would add speed and how much strength work I had to do at what point.'

David Platt set himself the goal of playing for England's first side after he had played for the Under-21s and then the England B team. Those experiences made him think that playing for the first squad was possible. Platt says:

'You have to set yourself a goal that is achievable. It has to be in touching distance. Once you have got it, nothing says you can't set yourself another goal. For nine or ten years that's what I have been doing. I said to myself, "I want to be an England regular, I want to go to Italy". You just go on and on, setting yourself a goal that you can focus on, that is achievable and that you have a drive and desire to get.'

When Platt scored for England in the World Cup he then set himself the goal of becoming England captain.

'I'd scored against Belgium and people were talking about me. I'd scored other goals in the World Cup too, and there was talk in the papers that there would be a new England

captain and there was talk that it would be me. So it became
a goal to become captain.'

Achieving that goal and captaining England for three years
gives Platt most satisfaction when looking back at his playing
career.

'The pinnacle of anybody's career is to play for his country,
but to go one step further and captain your country – for me,
that was the pinnacle. If I could only keep one thing that I
have achieved, it would be the England captaincy. To lead
your team out at Wembley was a tremendous feeling.'

THE ROLE OF THE COACH

While sporting champions have to set and be committed to
their own goals, the coach plays a vital part in helping them
achieve those goals.

Professor Graham Jones says that coaches play an important role in helping athletes to set goals because there is a fine
dividing line between having goals which are absolutely fantastic, and goals that are too ambitious and are therefore bad
goals. Coaches have an important role to play in helping performers keep their feet on the ground and focus on the things
that are important. Winning is important, but there are other
things that are going to help people win. Professor Jones says
he has come across too many coaches for whom the result has
been the all-important thing, with the consequence that they
have put too much pressure on their athletes.

When David Lloyd was running the Slater Scheme to train
boys showing early tennis talent, he realized that goal-setting
was an important tool. As a coach, he tried to encourage the
boys to set goals effectively.

'Every six months I made the boys write a list of their goals.
Then they had to come and talk to me about them. I would
ask them why they had chosen those goals. So they wrote

down their goals and we monitored them. I would try to get them to think more around the subject.

'With goals, it doesn't matter whether you are a sportsman or a businessman, you have to revisit them every six months minimum, because they will change. External circumstances might change and the goal might be unattainable and there's nothing worse than putting a goal that's unattainable because you just go downhill.

'There are also tasks as well as goals. I would link a goal with a task, so there's a ladder to go up to reach the goal.

'Sometimes I set myself really tough goals, but I know if you keep at it, you'll get pretty close.'

Lloyd trod carefully if a child wrote down a goal he thought unattainable. He says coaches must be very careful that the ambition burning in a youngster is not put out. On the other hand, some kids will say they have a certain goal just because they think that is what the coach wants to hear. They might say they want to win Wimbledon, when that doesn't really mean anything to them. Lloyd says that coaches therefore do need to dig deeply to make sure that the stated goal really is embedded in the youngster's heart.

Former national athletics coach Frank Dick has an uncompromising attitude to the importance of goal-setting, believing it absolutely essential. Athletes need to be clear about what their goals are in the coming year. If a 400m runner wants to win an Olympic gold, he needs to work out the performance required to achieve it – say 43.50 seconds. Then he needs to think about the consistent quality of performance and training required in the season in order for 43.50 seconds to be a realistic goal; the fitness parameter for that consistency; and the preparation plan detail to achieve the goal.

When thinking about the consistent quality of performance required, parameters need to be established in terms of the athlete's conditioning and techniques. Then the coach draws up the training plan, breaking it down into six-week cycles, and taking into account the competition programme. Controls need to be built in to test that the athlete is on track and making progress. Although the plan becomes very detailed, it has to be open to adjustment if the athlete performs unexpectedly well.

The plan needs to consider the support people required – the doctor, psychologist, physiotherapist, physiologist, biochemist. Any special training needs for the individual in question should be considered. Is there anything more that could help the person achieve this year's goals? The planning must be comprehensive.

Dick believes that coaches should be so attuned to their athletes and so focused on the detail of the training plan that they can predict how their athletes will perform at a particular competition during the season timetable. He says:

> 'I find it inexcusable if a coach can't tell me on Monday what he thinks his or her athlete is going to do on the Saturday. It's not good enough to say you are going to do a little bit better. If you really know your business, you should know to within a few hundredths of a second. Daley Thompson's lifetime best in 100m was 10.31 seconds prior to the 1986 European Championships in Stuttgart. Tests over 30m and 60m made 10.27 or 10.28 achievable. He ran 10.26.'

When choosing competitions tests during a season and when building up to a major championship, Dick believes those tests must be truly challenging. Otherwise, why bother with them? Dick says:

> 'The purpose of competition is to help you perform better. There's no point in finding competition you can beat. I was puzzled back in 2000 when the England football team went to play Malta as their last game before the start of the European Championships. Malta's a very passionate nation about football; in fact, they are an accomplished team, considering the population numbers. But what level of challenge did they really present for England? Hardly testing! That would be like Linford Christie racing local sprinters in preparation for the Olympics. You know that's

stupid. You find competition that challenges and pushes you on to even greater things. Otherwise, how do you become that champion?

'You sometimes see pretty useful athletes ducking out of competitions because they would like to have an easy outing to build their self-belief. Come on guys. You want to be the best in the world. If you don't beat someone this time, beat them next time. If it doesn't happen that time, beat them the time after that. You seek them out. You seek out people who are even better than you are and you keep going at them. You've got to keep the will to win there all the time. It's about your drive, your sense of purpose, your relentless determination to keep going for your goal. You're going to get there, so how do you get there? By being better than you are today. Athletes need to keep their minds on that. You may not guarantee the results at the end of it, because you've only got control over your performance. But if you keep on performing better, your chances of a result are a lot better than if you don't.'

Achieving a goal is a great feeling – for sporting champions as well as ordinary people. And like ordinary people, champions also often have heroes – people who have inspired them to aim high and give their all. But who are these heroes?

Analysis II

MOTIVATIONAL MATTERS

ACKNOWLEDGED SPORTING CHAMPIONS clearly need the physical talent and the trained skill to succeed, but they also need motivation to keep them going when times are tough. Something has to keep them training even when their limbs ache, it's 6 o'clock in the morning and they would rather be in bed. In Part II we looked at champions' motivations – what it is that drives them on.

CHAPTER 4

In Chapter 4: The Success Magnet, we found that many champions have a strong 'need' to win. Coming second simply isn't good enough. In particular, they want to win the really big occasions – world championships and the Olympics as compared to ordinary international contests.

Many sportspeople are motivated to put in the hard training required because they want to experience the feelings that come with being a winner. They are attracted towards the feelings of esteem and elation that come from winning gold. For some of our interviewees, achieving success in their sport as a child gave them a sense of esteem. Olympic swimmer Adrian Moorhouse was a small, shy child, but swimming made him a winner.

However, the emotions associated with winning vary from person to person. Some feel great elation; some describe feeling great relief that they have achieved their goals; many are moved to tears.

These differing emotions are not surprising given that, in simple terms, there are two different types of motivation: the desire to move 'towards' and 'away from' certain feelings. Champions who thrive on the feelings of elation are pulled towards those feelings; the desire to experience them again motivates them during the preparatory training required. However, many sportspeople are also motivated to train because they don't want to fail, or to let people down. Their drive is underpinned by needing to avoid feeling something. We looked at this group in more detail in Chapter 5: Fleeing Failure.

As Ceri Evans from mental conditioning specialists Gazing Performance explains, in practice most sportspeople are motivated by a mixture of the 'towards' and 'away from' drivers, though one theme may dominate at any particular time. The common denominator is the intensity of *emotion* that is involved in these drivers. For example, rugby players may want to win the World Cup, but the underlying significance of this will vary from player to player. The reason lies in the emotional associations. It may be that winning the World Cup will enable that rugby player to say, 'I am the best'. For another player winning the World Cup may mean they are part of a winning team and so they feel accepted, because they belong to that successful group. For other individuals the key factor may be that they are moving away from the feeling of letting anyone down. When the team wins, they feel they haven't disappointed anyone and the dominant feeling may be one of relief.

The champions we interviewed were strongly motivated because they wanted to enjoy certain feelings and they really didn't want to experience others. Without a strong emotional response to winning or losing, the people we talked to wouldn't be champions; they simply wouldn't have the motivation to do what needs to be done to achieve their goals.

Renzie Hanham from Gazing Performance points out that in a business environment it is useful to know what drives the members of your team. Are the goals of the group aligned with the drivers of the individuals involved? If not, then the likely result is disharmony and resistance to what you are trying to achieve. Similarly, in your personal relationships, if you and your partner don't share similar goals and drivers, what Renzie calls the 'themes' of each person's life will become quite different. Eventually this can create a wedge between the two of you, potentially driving you apart.

These drivers are closely related to how we define ourselves. Ceri Evans notes that people can define themselves in many different ways. An elite sportsman might define himself as 'the world champion' or 'the best in the UK'. Such status may be so important to their sense of self that they will endure great hardship to maintain it. The way that we define ourselves will generally change over time, as our lives develop and our priorities change. This process can have important implications for sportspeople as their careers progress, in the way that they come to define themselves more strongly in terms of the level of their achievement and ambition.

A final motivational force we found amongst our sporting champions was the desire to beat their own previous best performances. They weren't just competing against their competitors, but against themselves.

This kind of attitude is one that can be applied in all walks of life. You don't need to be competing in a sporting environment. You can compete against yourself to improve your performance at work, in your hobbies and anything else you want to do well.

Applications

- Think about times when you achieved something that meant a lot to you. Maybe you passed an exam, managed to hold a conversation successfully in a foreign language or gave your first major presentation. How did that make you feel? Were you elated? Did you feel like jumping up and down with joy? Were you simply relieved that you didn't let yourself down? In fact, you probably felt a bit of both, but was one stronger? By thinking about your reaction you can get a better understanding of what motivates you – 'towards' or 'away from' feelings.
- Think about something you want to achieve in future. What is it that motivates you? Do you want other people to acknowledge your achievement? Will you feel relief that you have done something you always said you would? Are there similarities with how you felt about the things you have achieved before?
- Whenever you decide to achieve something challenging, make a note of what it is that motivates you. Refer to it whenever you need a boost to keep you going.

CHAPTER 5

In Chapter 5: Fleeing Failure, we looked specifically at champions who were driven by the desire not to fail. For these people the emotions that came with being beaten felt so bad that they were highly motivated to do all they could to make sure they didn't have to suffer them.

For example, 400m champion Roger Black talks of the 'great pain' that he feels if he looks back and knows he didn't do something properly.

Sometimes it isn't just your own feelings that matter. Yachtswoman Ellen MacArthur hates to think she has let down all the people in the support team working with her; she feels she has to do well for their sakes.

Other people can also provide a motivating force for our sporting champions – by telling them they can't do something. For some people, being told you will fail provides huge motivation to prove that person wrong by succeeding. This was the case for Sally Gunnell early in her sporting career when she was told she would never be good enough to be a top hurdler.

Champions who are driven to avoid feelings of failure generally feel relief as the dominant emotion when they win. There is euphoria too, but relief is the major sensation.

As we noted in considering the findings in Chapter 4: The Success Magnet, the emotional response that comes from winning – or not losing – is absolutely key to the motivation of successful people. These feelings and emotions really matter. They can't be easily shrugged off or ignored. Without this strong emotional response, no one would spend hours every day practising a skill or improving fitness, perhaps in addition to holding down a full-time job. This would be madness, if it wasn't for the powerful emotional impact that becoming an Olympic medallist or winning Wimbledon has.

The same applies in everyday life, though perhaps on a less dramatic scale. Renzie Hanham from mental conditioning specialists Gazing Performance suggests that if we understand our drivers, how they relate to our emotions and underpin our motivations, then we can be more deliberate about the choices we make. This in turn will allow us to feel more in control of our lives.

Applications

- In the applications for Chapter 4: The Success Magnet, we suggested you recall the emotions you felt when achieving success in the past. Now try thinking about some goal or task you want to complete now. Imagine how you will feel having completed it. Imagine the feelings of joy and imagine how you will celebrate. Sense the wonderful feeling of relief you will have. (This is particularly relevant if the task is something you don't necessarily want to do, but need to do.) Revel in how good it feels, then think about the goal or task itself. Do you feel more motivated to achieve it now?

CHAPTER 6

Goals play an important part in motivating any athlete, a topic we considered in Chapter 6: Goals Galore. Goal-setting is in fact an invaluable tool for anyone seeking to achieve a particular ambition, be it a sporting challenge, a career ambition or a personal dream.

Renzie Hanham of mental conditioning specialists Gazing Performance says that having clear goals can help drive certain behaviours which can keep you motivated in the most difficult situations. It's not the goals themselves that are necessarily significant; it's what those goals represent, what significance they have for the individual. This significance 'drives' the individual to achieve the goals they have established. The more meaning the goals have, the more the individual will be driven to achieve them.

All the champions we spoke to set themselves goals. Many did so from an early age and it was something that they did naturally.

The goals that champions set are commonly divided into three types: outcome goals, which set the target, such as winning the gold medal: performance goals, such as the time required to win the race; and process goals, which address how that performance will be achieved – perhaps by focusing on a particular aspect of the technique involved.

By formalizing a goal and writing it down, you can develop a sense of commitment to achieving it. Once you have established the ultimate goal – the outcome goal – you can work backwards to establish the steps you need to complete to achieve it. The individual steps keep you focused on the processes you need to follow in order to achieve your ultimate goal, while the emotions associated with that ultimate goal keep you motivated when the going gets tough.

The goals that are set need to be realistic and achievable. If they are too hard, they will have no motivational impact. If they are too easy, then achieving them means nothing. They should be flexible and can be changed if your rate of development suddenly alters. In fact, goals should be reviewed regularly and adjusted as necessary.

Coaches can play an invaluable role in helping emerging champions to establish realistic goals, and in ensuring that the individual really does want to achieve that goal. If the thought of achieving the goal doesn't trigger strong emotions, it is a waste of time to try to achieve it.

Renzie Hanham stresses the importance of alignment between an individual's goals and values. When there is mis-alignment between the goals and values that athletes have, they often sabotage their own performance. In contrast, the greater the alignment, the greater the chance of success.

Top sportspeople generally use goal-setting much more effectively than people with non-sporting ambitions. In the business world, for example, people often overcomplicate matters by trying to achieve too many things at once, rather than focusing on three or four key objectives. Most sportspeople have far more clarity about their goals. That clarity is important for maintaining motivation and focusing on what needs to be done to achieve the desired goals. We can all learn from sporting champions by trying to be more precise about what it is we are aiming to do and the steps we must take to succeed.

Secondly, top sportspeople typically are far more disciplined than other people in terms of completing the processes they need to complete in order to achieve their goals. As Ceri Evans from Gazing Performance says, many people performing in domains outside sport, such as business, aren't as organized as elite sportspeople. Some initiate good processes by doing a lot of work on outcomes and targets, but then don't follow it up on the preparatory work. Goals are only useful if you have discipline behind them.

Applications

- Identify one or more outcome goals or ambitions that you have. This could relate to your work or private life. It might be to achieve a promotion or even to change careers. Perhaps you want to be able to move up your squash ladder or be able to paint a picture of your child – one that you would be proud to hang on your wall.
- Take each goal and think about what you need to do to be able to achieve it – your performance goals. For example, if you want to be promoted to sales manager for your area, what kind of performance do you need to deliver? Perhaps you need to increase your sales by a certain amount or demonstrate your ability to manage other people.
- Think about the process goals that will support your outcome and performance goals. If you need to display staff management skills, what does this mean? Do you need any extra training to be able to delegate effectively or coach members of your team well? Identify the things you need to do to start working towards your ultimate outcome goals.
- Set your goals in a timeframe. When do you want to achieve that promotion? Work backwards to establish the timescale you need in order to achieve the supporting steps along the way.
- Review your plan. Is it realistic? Is it too easy? If you need to adjust the timescale, do so. Your aim should be to come up with a plan that inspires you to achieve it and that you believe you can achieve.
- Consider taking advice from someone with relevant experience whose opinions you trust. They may be able to comment on whether your performance and process goals are appropriate.

Part III
MENTAL TRAINING

Chapter 7

MENTAL REHEARSAL

VISUALIZATION IS AN IMPORTANT TOOL that any athlete can use when preparing for competition. Champion sportspeople use it expertly to give themselves the greatest chance of performing at their absolute best when it counts.

WHAT IS VISUALIZATION?

Visualization is the process of seeing yourself doing what it is you need to do – whether running a winning race, throwing a record-breaking javelin distance or kicking the perfect penalty. To make the visualization as powerful as possible, you should be seeing the experience through your own eyes – rather than watching yourself as if on a screen. You should also engage all your senses.

For this reason sports psychologist John Syer prefers the term 'mental rehearsal' to 'visualization', because visualization suggests that the process or experience is totally visual, when it is not. The most important component is kinaesthetic.

Recalling the 'feel' of the action is vital. This is an aspect that multiple javelin champion Steve Backley learnt when working with a sports psychologist. He has always used visualization to great effect when preparing for competition, but he has improved his technique over the years. Backley says:

> *'I was lucky – I did it automatically as a kid and I've always been quite visual. Then I met a psychologist, Dave Collins, around seven years ago. He picked up on the fact that I did visualize but that I did it externally, as if watching myself on TV. Dave was more feelings based. We did a lot more on the rhythm of the run, how it feels, the surging of acceleration and so on.'*

The trick to visualization, according to 400m runner Roger Black, is not to see yourself doing the desired action, but to see inside yourself as if you are doing it. As Black describes it, you are not looking at yourself, but you are 'actually in yourself, feeling'.

Black practised his visualization of a race so that it became extremely vivid.

> *'I could lie down and see it, hear it, smell it. It never included the results, though. I believed that I could only influence my performance, not the results. My performance was under my control, the result wasn't. The magic was to get the performance right; the result would usually follow.'*

Sports psychologist Ian Lynagh feels that using visualization techniques, or mental rehearsal, is an essential part of any sporting preparation. As he explains, most of the things we do in our lives start with us imagining them in our heads. What the mind imagines usually creates a capacity for the body to do it. Therefore it makes sense to train athletes to visualize their golf swing, kicking the ball or whatever it is they are going to do. They can even visualize achieving their goals.

Anyone who enjoys watching athletics will have seen competitors using the technique of mental rehearsal during competitions. When high jumpers, for example, are preparing to jump they mentally run through what they are going to do just before they do it. As Lynagh says, you can see them talking themselves through the jump one step at a time – setting off, building up momentum, hitting the board and taking off. While they go through this mental rehearsal you can often see their bodies moving. As Lynagh explains, this is an ideo-motor response. In other words, the idea of the movement produces a motor response.

Former national athletics coach Frank Dick believes that athletes should adapt the basic visualization process to ensure that it works effectively for them. Although the visualization process can be made to sound complicated, it isn't. Dick has found that each athlete has their own sense of what visualization is. When someone is trying to learn a new technique, but finding it difficult, visualizing it, or as Dick says 'feeling it with words', can help. He recalls a long jumper he worked with. When she described how she geared herself up before a jump she said she liked to sense she was 'collecting', just as she would 'collect' horses. Dick says that her background included horse riding, so using that term worked for her.

Dick explains that choosing the right word is important for giving the right mental image or sensation of what the athlete is trying to do. He explains:

> *'A lot of coaches used to talk about "driving" off the bend in the 200 metres, but that's not a very effective thing to do. If you think "drive", you think about a longer period of contact with the ground. But longer contact with the ground actually slows you down. An expression Don Quarrie used was "lift off the bend" – so you think about touching the ground very lightly. That actually gives you a sense of acceleration. It's not just a mental thing, it's a factual thing. You accelerate off the bend, but that acceleration's not done the*

*way you would normally accelerate from the blocks. It's
done by being light and using a different configuration of
sprinting technique.'*

POSITIVE RESULTS

Visualization is an important element of Neuro-Linguistic
Programming (NLP), which is looked at in more depth in
Chapter 8. NLP trainer Graham Shaw explains that the reason
why visualization works from an NLP perspective is that the
mind doesn't actually know the difference between a real or
an imagined experience.

Shaw recalls a story told him by his skiing instructor. A man
turned up for a ski course a year after attending the previous
one – but he had vastly improved during the year's gap. The
instructor asked him where he had been skiing in between
times, and was told he hadn't skied at all. What the guy had
done was to think about skiing and he had found that he could
remember the route he used to ski down. He told the instructor he'd skied down it a hundred times in his head. Of course,
in his head, he had skied it perfectly. According to Shaw, if
we imagine an experience powerfully enough, we have the
opportunity to programme our minds to do something successfully every time.

Shaw says that one of the ways visualization helps athletes
is by creating positive 'filters'. Everyone automatically creates
their own filters through which they view the world. These
filters can be supportive or limiting, depending on the individual's past experiences and response to those experiences.
Shaw explains:

*'In life we experience the world in different ways, so we create
our own mental maps. We create pictures and sounds in our
minds, self-talk, and feelings that are all component parts
of our internal experience. In NLP we call that your "map".
One of the reasons people often don't communicate well is
because they're on different maps.*

'We filter the world and our experiences and create different maps. That means we don't notice everything. If two people see the same film they might notice different bits or the music would have different effects on them. How does that apply to sport?

'Say two people decide to learn tennis. Player number one has begun to talk to himself about learning tennis. He turns up for his lesson and he's already said to himself in his mind 100 times "I was never any good at tennis at school, therefore I can't learn tennis. I was always last in the running race and I'm no good at sports." Even before he begins his lesson he's got a set of filters on the world; it's as if he's put a special pair of glasses on and he sees everything through those. He starts the tennis lesson and hits three balls over the net and seven into the net. He says to himself, "That's awful. I've hit seven balls into the net." That's what he noticed. He started with the belief that he was no good at tennis and now he's reinforced it. Then he notices how he hits even more balls into the net.

'Another player comes along who has never played tennis. He thinks, "I've learned a lot of other stuff and I can't see why I can't learn this." He also hits seven balls into the net and three over. He says to himself, "I've hit three balls over already. I wonder if I can get five over? Perhaps I can learn this."

'So visualization works because you set your filters up in advance.'

RE-EDITING THE PAST

Mental rehearsal can also be used to minimize the impact of poor performances and negative associations. Sports psychologist John Syer says that visualization can be used to re-edit a bad mistake. This is helpful because if someone has made some bad mistake, they may unconsciously replay it mentally, which actually makes it more likely to happen again in a similar situation.

Syer explains how he leads a visualization exercise with athletes.

'I ask for the background, what immediately preceded the action to be visualized. I then lead a relaxation, followed by the beginning of the visualization. I ask the athlete to be aware of the scene, who is there, the colours, the sounds, any movement and the atmosphere. I then repeat the beginning of the story I have just heard, in the present tense. I then ask the athlete to continue the action, aware of how it feels to perform like this, and to move one finger on completion.'

When the person has finished the visualization, Syer doesn't ask them to open their eyes immediately. Instead he asks them to come up with a verbal description that is linked to the visualization. For example, Syer might ask the athlete to complete the sentence 'I feel as if I ...' When they are ready and can complete the sentence, they open their eyes.

'That can be turned into an affirmation. An affirmation is a sentence that is connected to a past, positive experience, begins with the word "I" and is in the present tense. It can be repeated internally or written on to a piece of paper that is put into one's bag or wallet or stuck on to the fridge door. The affirmation is connected to the visualization.'

Recalling that affirmation associates the individual again with the positive outcome, encouraging them to anticipate and achieve the positive result they want.

VISUALIZATION IN PRACTICE

Modern pentathlon Olympic gold medallist Dr Stephanie Cook worked with a sports psychologist once a week when she was training. They would work on various mental aspects of the sport, including visualization techniques. This meant that when she learnt something new in a coaching session, she was able to rehearse it mentally for herself before actually putting it into practice. 'You can put things into practice much more easily when you have gone over them in your head a few times,' she says.

Dr Cook practised her visualization regularly.

'It's the sort of thing you might do at odd moments when you're waiting around – say you're waiting for a fencing lesson. You can sit down quietly and go through a few things. But it is important to set a time when you will do it as well. I would make a conscious effort to make that time.'

Michael Lynagh, former Australian rugby captain and renowned fly-half, would rehearse his kicking mentally the night before a match. He would do so having already visited the ground he would be playing on and practised kicking in the local conditions. He practised kicks at Twickenham the afternoon before the 1991 World Cup final.

'That night, when I was going to sleep, I would mentally rehearse those kicks. I had the picture of the ground in my mind. I even knew the publicity boards. I knew what the posts were like. I could visualize all that.'

Lynagh had begun using mental rehearsal techniques early on in his career, back in the early 1980s.

'I have done it for a long time. It was part of my pre-match routine. When I was doing a mental rehearsal I would lie down and I could see lots of fine detail – even seeing the referee giving a penalty. It would include the position, the people in front of you, the sand boy coming out and giving me some sand, setting the ball up, walking back, visualizing where the ball was going to go, then coming in and kicking it and seeing the result. I would see the linesman putting the flag up. It would take a while to go through it all. I could see it very clearly.'

Lynagh found it important to 'feel' the process of the kick as well as see it. He says you have to involve your senses in sport. The more you involve, the better. He says you need to feel it, see it, hear it – use all your senses.

Visualization is essential for success in motorsport too, as Ron Dennis, boss of the McLaren racing team explains.

'Most drivers will visualize not just the course, but every blade of grass. For Monte Carlo, the top drivers will also be driving it in their dreams. It's so fast. It calls on every sense. They'll be visualizing the things they have to do to become fluid. With a top driver the whole process is fluid, in harmony. There is a tranquillity about them, a rhythm.'

Lawrence Dallaglio, England rugby captain, starts visualizing the competition he's up against during the last few days before the match. He puts himself in the match environment, so that when the whistle blows he knows he's been there before.

'You can teach yourself visualization, but it's something you have to practise. You have to coach yourself. It's a whole new world – how the body reacts to the mind. But there is a lot to be said for walking around a rugby pitch two or three days before you play on it, and visualizing yourself doing everything perfectly – making a perfect pass, a perfect line-out and perfect tackles. Seeing yourself in the arena. Then when you go home, when you have got a bit of time to yourself to meditate, you might do the whole process again. As a result, when you go back on game day, you are not there for the first time and you know you are going to play well because you already have done.'

Sprinter John Regis used visualization and mental rehearsal when preparing for a major championship.

'I'd always have two or three days beforehand just rehearsing the race in my head. I would rehearse every facet of the race until I got bored, and then I did it some more. I did it

*so that when I got to that particular situation, I didn't need
to think about anything. I just did it.*

*'All I did was visualize winning. It didn't matter what
lane it was because I knew what I had to do. I was imagining the perfect race and the feeling I got when I was running
the perfect race. When that happens it's called being in the
zone, because you just don't seem able to lose or run badly.
Even if you try to run badly, you can't because you're so
tuned to what you should be doing and how you're sup-
posed to perform, no matter what's going on around you.'*

When on the blocks, waiting for the gun to go off, Regis kept
his mind blank.

*'I'm just thinking, "On any sound – go". I already know
what I'm going to do, so I don't worry about it. When the
gun goes, my body will take over with what it's been trained
to do. The gun is the trigger that brings back the memory of
all the mental visualization I'd done before, two days ago,
a day ago, even two hours before.'*

SCENARIO PLANNING

One great benefit from using visualization or mental rehearsal
techniques is that they enable the individual to prepare for
unexpected eventualities or unfamiliar situations. As NLP
trainer Graham Shaw explains, visualization enables people
to create a sense of familiarity in new situations, thus remov-
ing the shock of the new. Even if you don't know exactly what's
going to happen, you can practise reacting to unexpected
events. For example, a presenter with a business audience
who doesn't want to handle awkward questions can imagine in
advance how he's handling the questions to which he doesn't
know the answer. He can imagine himself doing so successfully, and so improve his chances of actually performing well
at the real event.

Sports psychologist Professor Graham Jones says that close
to a race athletes should be visualizing in a very positive way,

drawing on past successes so that they are building confidence and belief as the race approaches. A few days beforehand, you should go through all the 'what ifs'. You identify all the different scenarios and what might go wrong and you work through them. This helps you to be thoroughly prepared for anything that happens.

Early in her career, Olympic hurdles gold medallist Sally Gunnell simply used visualization the night before a race. Then, in the run up to the 1992 Olympics, she began using visualization much more intensively and placing herself in a wide variety of different situations. She estimates that from October 1991, leading into Barcelona in 1992, she would go through the race on average 11 or 12 times a day.

David Hemery, former 400m hurdle Olympic gold medallist, helped Gunnell with the technique when she met him a couple of times in the year before the 1992 Olympics. Hemery was so expert at his visualization and experienced it so vividly that he could actually make himself sick at the end of visualizing a race.

'Hemery taught me how to visualize, starting around September 1991. He told me I had to visualize myself in every situation that could happen in that one race – the Olympic final. He taught me to make sure I went through the race including every scenario – whether I was in lane one with tight bends, whether I hit a hurdle, and seeing my competitors outside me. I had to make sure I got through the situation, corrected myself and got back into the stride pattern, making sure that I ran that perfect race.

'The key was making sure I crossed the line first in every situation. I'd find my brain telling me negative thoughts, but I had to see that tape and stop it – rewind it, making sure I crossed the line first every single time.

'I did it repeatedly during the day. I'd be sitting down at home watching television, or maybe I was training – but I'd go through the situation. It was hard at times to start with, but then I found it began to come naturally and became a way of life.'

Repeated visualization gave Gunnell the comfort of familiarity, whatever happened in the race.

> *'It felt comfortable; it felt familiar. If something happened – if I hit a hurdle or came off the eighth hurdle and wasn't in the lead – it felt familiar and I knew I should get back in the race. The race that I won – the 1992 Olympic final – I had visualized so many times. I included every situation and different athletes, whether they were on the inside or the outside of me.'*

The visualization technique became so much a way of life that Gunnell still uses it, even though her athletics career is over.

> *'I use it, for example, when I'm going to do a big talk. I've just done one to 5000 people, which scared the life out of me. But I visualized myself standing on the stage, delivering the perfect speech and people enjoying what I was saying. It really helped and allowed me to control my nerves. I still find that live TV gets nerve-racking, but I visualize myself beforehand talking and feeling confident. You can use the technique for whatever you are doing in life. If you want to lose weight you can visualize how you want to look. So many people on diets don't actually see themselves how they want to be, getting into certain clothes. You can draw on that picture on days when you lose your motivation.'*

Adrian Moorhouse, Olympic gold medallist in the 100m breast-stroke, also used visualization to enhance his own competitive performance. He used to imagine various 'what if' scenarios – not necessarily positive ones.

> *'My race is two lengths. So, what if at halfway you are in last place? What do you do? I would visualize the start of the race and then swimming through and coming to a success-ful outcome. I would visualize different scenarios during the race, but it was always a successful outcome. The idea*

*was that whatever the eventuality, you'd been there before
so that it wasn't a worry – you knew what you would do.*

*'I was also a big fan of visualizing the race with a stop-
watch – starting the watch at the same time that I started
the visualization and trying to get the same time as when I
swam. I used to get within half a second.*

*'I also used to visualize training. I would invent training
partners swimming next to me. I imagined when we were
kicking, leg kicks, it really hurt them.'*

When the 100m breaststroke final arrived in Seoul in 1988,
Moorhouse found that his visualization practice paid off.

*'I remember swimming into the first turn, touching the wall
and going under the water. I remember having a quick look
and thinking, "Shit, I'm behind, but I've visualized what
I've got to do now. I've got to catch that Russian guy. The
same thing happened in my visualization. I was behind in
the first length and I caught him." I remember thinking I'd
left it too late. But I thought, "Keep going, hold the stroke,
hold the stroke …" and I remember it being very painful.'*

Moorhouse stole the lead and won gold – by a hundredth of
a second.

When yachtsman Sir Chay Blyth's catamaran capsized
at Cape Horn, Blyth put into practice the actions he had
rehearsed beforehand.

*'You've gone through exercises in the event that you capsize
– what you've got to do – so the actions just click in. It's like
if your clutch goes on the car, you just pull into the side of
the road and put your indicators on. You know what you've
got to do in that situation and you just click into it. There's
never any panic.'*

Three times Olympic gold rowing medallist Matthew Pinsent
knows the importance of mental rehearsal to prepare for any
eventuality in the race.

'You mentally rehearse all the time. You imagine what the race is going to be like, what the opposition is going to do and what the feeling on the start line is going to be like. You imagine the weather conditions, the lake, the crowd and then you superimpose on that any amount of race outcomes or eventualities. You're constantly asking yourself, What happens if we do this? What happens if we make a good start? What happens if we make a bad start? What happens if New Zealand are half a length up on us when we don't expect them to be? What happens if we get within 20 strokes of the line and we're not leading? You go over and over them again and again. It's an illusion to think that you only think about winning because it's not true; you think about losing the whole time and you try and examine what the factors are that are going to make you lose or what mistakes you could make that would make you lose.

'Then it's important that if you ever don't know how you would deal with a scenario, that you talk to the other guys in the crew. There's very little communication that can go on during a race, so you've got to be able to deal with every eventuality with a very limited number of words or calls. The closer the competition gets, the more often you have these discussions. During the heat, the semi-final and the final, you're looking at the opposition and trying to figure out what's going to happen and who might have something up their sleeve.'

Having a number of plans is vital to cope with all eventualities. As Pinsent says, you can't rely on the A plan all the time. If you *can* win the gold medal with the A plan, that's great, but more often than not you're pretty quickly down to plan B and then C. For Pinsent, the transition isn't panic stricken. He says:

'It's more like, "Okay, this is what they're doing, so this is what we're doing." If that doesn't work, we've got something else. You've got multilayers of tactics and confidence and ideas; as soon as you run out of ideas or you're taken by surprise by something, then you're in trouble. Then you're

> *being defensive or waiting for them to make a mistake to*
> *hand the impetus back to you again.'*

Javelin champion Steve Backley realizes the importance of being prepared for unexpected eventualities. He says it is essential to have a solution for any possible problem that could arise.

> *'For the 2002 Commonwealth Games in Manchester I*
> *made a trip up to make sure the run up was long enough*
> *and that there were no obstructions. Sometimes there's a*
> *drain, for example. One exercise I do is to make a snag*
> *list and write down anything and everything that could go*
> *wrong – for example, that the freezer breaks when I'm away*
> *or someone breaks into the house or my shoe lace snaps on*
> *the run-up.*
>
> *'I make a list of anything that can happen and then over*
> *three months come up with answers. I do that every year. I*
> *came a cropper once because there was one thing I hadn't*
> *put on the list. It was in Florida. I underestimated how hot*
> *it would be. I knew it would be hot, but didn't realize what*
> *effect it would have on my contact with the javelin.'*

This kind of preparation may seem like common sense, but it can still set champions apart from the rest. It isn't just the fact they make these preparations that counts, but the detail and quality involved. In the next chapter we look at some particular techniques that can help champions perform at their best, when they want.

Chapter 8

ANCHORS AND TRIGGERS

WHEN TRAINING THE MIND FOR COMPETITION, top athletes know that they can learn ways of creating certain desired mental states. In this way they can improve their ability to remain focused, to stay calm or to increase their determination – whatever the state they need to help them perform well.

NLP

This type of training is used in Neuro-Linguistic Programming, or NLP. As the name indicates, NLP is to do with the mind, language and programming: how to programme your mind for success. It was developed in the 1970s by Richard Bandler and John Grinder.

NLP trainer Graham Shaw explains that NLP is the study of what successful people do. In fact, NLP could be described as the art and science of human excellence. One of the principal uses of NLP is to model excellence. As Shaw explains, that essentially means that an NLP practitioner could take anyone in any field – an athlete, a footballer or a saleswoman – and analyse what it is they do that makes the difference in what they are doing. It might be to do with their sense of identity, what they believe about themselves, their values, what their skills and capabilities are, and their behaviours. Also, Shaw says, their environment has an impact. People who are successful tend to have all those elements in alignment. NLP therefore enables you to learn from anyone who is very good at something. Shaw says:

> 'You could take David Beckham and look at what he physically does, what he believes about himself, what his sense of identity is, what he does and what the component parts of that are that make the difference in terms of him being successful in pressurized situations. What is it he does that is merely idiosyncratic? That's not necessarily the bit you want to copy; that's just their foible.
>
> 'You often find that there are certain key pieces that make the difference. It could be physical, or to do with mental strategy, with visualization or with how they prepare. You then look at the person you want to transfer those skills to and you create their own kind of model. It's not going to be exactly the same. But hopefully you have enough pieces in there that it's going to make a difference to them.'

NLP techniques overlap with other areas of sports psychology. For example, NLP involves goal-setting, visualization and managing your state – getting psyched up or keeping nerves at a level that supports performance, rather than hampering it.

ANCHORS AND TRIGGERS

NLP provides a technique for creating desired states, such as a feeling of confidence. This technique is called 'anchoring'.

If someone says they have never felt confident on the starting line, that may be true, but they probably have felt confident in another situation. NLP enables someone to draw on that other experience and transfer it to the experience where they need it. Shaw explains:

'With NLP you would ask the person to think of a time when they felt really confident. As a coach, you could say, "Go back to a time when you felt really confident. It might be on holiday, at school or at work. A time when you felt you could do anything. Be there now. Are you there now?"'

Shaw says it is important to use the present tense when speaking to the individual who is recalling the experience. To help the person recreate the past sensations fully, you can ask questions such as: What are you seeing? What's the picture like? What are you hearing? Are the sounds loud or quiet? In this way, Shaw says, you can build up what are called the submodalities – the finer distinctions of the experience. When the experience becomes more real the physiology of the person changes; the person's breathing may change, for example. This is a sign that tells you they are really back in the experience and reliving it fully.

The aim is to get the person into an associated experience, rather than a dissociated one. This means that the person is seeing the experience through their own eyes, rather than watching themselves having the experience. They are feeling the same sensations they felt before, in the same way.

When the individual is fully experiencing the desired state it is possible to create an 'anchor' that becomes associated with the state. This could be achieved by simply squeezing a certain finger, or touching them on a certain point on their shoulder. If the anchor is firmly established, it is possible to 'trigger' the desired state at will and on command in future – simply by squeezing the same finger.

Anchors can take many forms. They can be words, memories, images, feelings or even pieces of clothing. Shaw says:

'When you go for an interview you might put on a particular tie because that tie makes you feel great. That's an anchor. You might put a piece of music on in the car when going to a difficult meeting because it buoys you up a little.'

Once you know what triggers work to create positive states for you, you can use them deliberately when needed. You can trigger them at will.

Shaw recalls an example of a word-based anchor told to him by a sports commentator.

'A basketball player had an anchor that he used in big tournaments so that he could put balls in the basket. He previously was very nervous. In training he could always put balls in the basket, but he couldn't always do it on the real court.

'So he was asked what feeling he would like to have in those situations on the basketball court and to recall a time when he had experienced that feeling in the past. He remembered a time when he was at the beach, sitting with his girlfriend on a wall overlooking the sea and eating soft ice cream. He said he felt great and that was how he wanted to feel on the basketball court. He was asked to get that feeling and then think of a word that would bring it back. His word was "soft ice". When he said "soft ice" to himself, he went back to that feeling. That association was built into him.

'When he went out onto the basketball court and the fans were screaming at him and he had to take a free shot, he could say "soft ice" to himself and he went into a different state. He created that sense of peace.'

Former 400m champion Roger Black used to listen to music for inspiration before a race, choosing the music he needed to create the desired mental state. This music was his trigger, but it took him some time to find out what music created the most appropriate mental state for him.

'Lyrics of songs inspire me. I listened to certain songs before I ran and some of them were really motivating for me. The lyric that motivated me most was written by a band I was a big fan of when I was younger, called Aztec Camera. A guy called Roddy Frame wrote all the songs. There was a lyric in one of his songs that really crystallized everything for me and I played it all the time. It said: "The secret is silver, it's to shine and to never simply survive." I always thought, "If I am going to do this I am going to shine and not just simply survive, not just do it because I am good at it." That song had a big effect on me. He was right because I got a silver medal!'

Sports psychologist John Syer works with sportspeople to help them develop useful triggers. Syer explains that triggers are a way of providing an association. For example, when you evoke an image or touch something it is often related to a particular feeling. However, when Syer is working with an athlete, the process is the other way round. Syer says:

'I ask what feeling they want in a particular situation. Working with cyclists, they may say that the feeling they want at the beginning of the race is different to the feeling they want when they are two thirds of the way up a steep hill. Once I know what feeling is important for the athlete in a given situation, I look at the triggers. I ask for the situations that evoke that feeling. What people? What clothes? What music?'

The same technique can be used in many situations. NLP trainer Graham Shaw, for example, uses it to help youngsters who get too nervous before taking exams. He asks them to choose the resource they want to have available to them in the situation. This might be a sense of calm, for example, or a feeling of relaxation with a bit of anticipation thrown in. The resource identified, Shaw asks the person to identify a situation in the past when they had that resource – when they experienced the desired state. He says:

'You ask them to go there and fully experience it, so they can step forward into it, visualize it, imagine it, experience it fully. Then you get them to step back out again. Then get them to go back in. You do that about four or five times. Then they can more or less do it when they want. They can access that resource.'

Before relying on the anchor in a real situation, Shaw recommends giving it a test to check it works. Take the teenager who is nervous about exams and develops an anchor for calmness. He can test this anchor by imagining walking into the exam room and then asking himself how he feels. If he feels nervous, he should try using his anchor and then ask himself how he feels again. If he feels calm, the technique has worked.

As we have said, triggers can take many different forms. Music can be a valuable trigger for encouraging creative thought. Shaw says:

'If you want to improve at a stroke your ability to study, or to be creative when you have to write a project, play some baroque music in the background very quietly. Baroque music goes at a rhythm of about 60 beats per minute, which roughly equates to the average heart rate. It slows down the heart rate and increases blood flow to the brain. It also begins to increase the flow or the doorway between the left and right sides of the brain. Why is that helpful? It puts you in a kind of trance. You find you're able to focus and you get into the flow. You're able to come up with lots of ideas very easily. And if you've got to learn something, that's the sort of music you want in the background.'

PRACTICAL USE

Breaststroke gold medallist Adrian Moorhouse worked with a sports psychologist during his career, learning about the power of the mind and techniques for manipulating the body with the mind. Part of this involved looking at ways for dealing with pain, and also for turning pain into a trigger to release extra adrenalin.

> '*I worked on this quite a lot before the World Champion-ships. I did a lot of trigger work related to pain, so that when it hit me, that was my trigger for "go for it". It was my trigger for: "The pain will release a surge of adrenalin in me and I will be the fastest swimmer in that pool." I actually felt myself lift in the water when it happened.*'

Dr Stephanie Cook also found triggers useful when she was competing in modern pentathlon, which requires completing five events during the course of a day.

> '*There's not much time to prepare between each event. You go directly from one to the next and you have to be able to switch straight away into the next mode. So I certainly used to use triggers. For example, every time I went to fence and put my mask down, that was a trigger for a certain mental state. That would be my cue to focus entirely on what I was doing and to forget all the distractions around me. It was a similar idea with putting on my goggles and getting up onto the blocks before the swimming event. These were all triggers.*'

In order for these triggers to become automatic, Cook had to practise them regularly.

> '*Unless you've practised something like that, you can't expect it to suddenly work in competition. When you go to a competition you're not actually expecting to do anything completely out of the ordinary. The chances are that you may; people end up surprising themselves because of that extra adrenalin. They might run that bit faster. But at the end of the day, you're not going to suddenly change what you do in practice. So you're not trying to do anything different; you're trying to perform to your potential – and you should be training at your potential as well. For me, that's*

how you go into competitions. You have the confidence to know what you're capable of doing – and that's what you're trying to achieve. Hopefully you'll do a bit better.'

Anchors and triggers can be used to create the right mental state in training, as well as when competing. If you don't have the right mental state when training, it doesn't have the same effect. Former Sunderland manager Howard Wilkinson says:

'We've got to get footballers to recognize that preparing for training is as important as preparing for a match. If you're going to maximize your training there's a warm-up period mentally and physically. The best preparation for getting the most out of your training is not to turn up at five to ten, throw your kit on and take a call on your mobile phone. You have your living zone and your training zone and in between there's a zone where you go from one to the other. You do that physically when you go out on the pitch. But mentally, the warm-up has to be done before that. It's something we've got to educate players about. If you're going to get the most out of training, your brain has got to be in training mode when you start.'

Getting the best out of training also requires players to try to recreate mentally the conditions they would face in a real game. Wilkinson says: 'If it's Friday morning and I've said there's to be no tackling, you've still got to train as if there is tackling.'

Mental training, and in particular techniques such as anchors and triggers, enables sporting champions to boost their performances. In the next chapter we look more widely at how elite sportspeople train their minds and bodies to cope with the pressure of competition.

Chapter 9

PREPARING FOR PRESSURE

WINNING RACES OR SCORING MATCH-WINNING GOALS doesn't come without some degree of pressure. The top quality sportspeople are those who show themselves able – time and again – to rise to the occasion and hold their nerve when it really counts. In fact, they thrive on that pressure – and they train themselves to make sure they perform well under it.

LEARNING TO HANDLE PRESSURE

Sports psychologist John Syer explains that excitement and anxiety are the same sort of emotion. An athlete learns that discomfort is necessary to a good performance. Sportsmen need to be excited and it is possible to turn anxiety into excitement. Syer says:

*'I was in a plane crash once and as a result I didn't fly for
a long time. But I eventually found a strategy for dealing
with my fear. This was to pay precise attention to my sensations in the moment. Fritz Perls, the colourful co-founder
of Gestalt Therapy, used to say "when you have one foot in
the past [what happened] and one foot in the future [what
might happen] you are pissing on the present." Once I'd
mastered this, I discovered that each time the plane I was
in was about to take off, I was excited. I had found a way to
redefine my sensations I was experiencing.'*

Professor Graham Jones has completed research that shows
the importance of dealing with the pressure of competition.
He says that thriving on the pressure of competition is a must
for top sporting champions. They know that the pressure is
going to be there and know they can handle it. They accept that
anxiety is inevitable and know they can cope with it. As Professor Jones says, you know it's going to be tough, you know there
are going to be times when you don't want to be there but you
come through because you've done it before.

In the course of his research Professor Jones has found that
elite and non-elite sportspeople experience the same things
in terms of physiological build-up, but elite performers interpret that differently to non-elite performers. The first group
experience facilitative anxiety, while the second experience
debilitative anxiety. In other words, Professor Jones says, elite
performers see what's happening to them in a very positive
way.

*'You might, for example, have a 100m sprinter who has a
massive physiological build-up. A sprinter came to me once
saying, "I don't want this, I don't like it. I want you to help
me relax and calm myself down." I said, "That's fine, but
let's think about what you're doing. The hundred metres is
about explosive power. What your body is doing is building
itself up to help you produce that. So I can help you compose yourself a little bit, but you don't want to lose that stuff*

either. So let's think about the way you think about it, and see that's it's actually helping you."

'That sprinter, during the build-up, began thinking that "this is brilliant – let's have some more" and that the build-up was helping. It was just a completely different psyche to the same physiological response.'

As Professor Jones explains, what matters is how people interpret what is happening to them. If you put yourself in a stressful situation you can interpret it in one of two ways. You can see it as a real threat and get all the negative things that go with that, or you can interpret it as a real opportunity – you can look forward to it and accept it. The same things happen to you, but you have a completely different response. For example, Professor Jones says, you may not have got enough sleep the night before a major event, but that's OK. You can interpret it as meaning that you know the event is important and you are focused on your performance in it.

THRIVING UNDER PRESSURE

Former Australian fly-half Michael Lynagh was one of the greatest ever rugby kickers. For him, extreme pressure was a normal part of his sporting life. The whole match result could hinge on his ability to get the ball between the posts. Lynagh recalls one such situation when he was playing for Queensland against Ireland at Ballymore, Brisbane.

'The full-time siren had gone and we received a penalty to win – and that wasn't an easy one. Nothing else mattered but me kicking that goal and nobody else could have an influence on the match. I remember saying afterwards, "Yes, that's why you are a goal kicker".

'That time I got it, but I have missed kicks as well and that's pretty tough. But that's what you are there for. That's actually the performance. Performing under pressure, making decisions that influence outcomes, making actions

*that influence outcomes – that's one of the great things
about sport.'*

When putting together his dream team, former England rugby
head coach Clive Woodward looked for players who would, as
a group, rise to triumph in pressurized occasions.

*'You've got to try and find those players – and you do need
15 of them – who are absolutely going to rise to the occasion. Say it's a World Cup final, we're five points down and
we've got a scrum on their line. Is their mindset going to be
"Yes, fantastic, this is our moment", or "Oh my God"?'*

Anyone in the 'Oh my God' camp shouldn't have expected to
put on an England shirt in the near future.

Sprinter John Regis says he always felt under pressure
before a big race – a championship that came round once every
four years. When competing on those occasions he knew that
he had one chance to get it right. Everything before the big
race was just fine tuning and didn't matter. As Regis says, if you
made a mistake in the big race, you had another four years to
wait. That in itself created a lot of pressure.

How people cope with that pressure is a key factor in determining whether they become a champion or not. Champions
relish the chance to rise to the occasion when it matters, Regis
says.

*'You want to be in a pressure cooker situation. You want
to be there and to show the world that you can rise to the
occasion, even if you've had a bad season. For the champion, the only race that means anything is the big one. In
the others he could come fourth or fifth, but he knows he's
preparing for the one big race. I knew that I wanted to be at
my best for the European Championships, the Commonwealth Games, the World Championships, the Olympics.
The rest was irrelevant. People don't remember that John
had a great race in Zurich. To me that's what makes a
champion – it's the person who can raise their game when*

everybody's there competing in a major championship. I wanted to be the man standing tall at the top.

'Talent gives people an ability to perform, but if all the guys on the line have the same amount of talent, then it's the mental strength that determines who crosses the line first. It's the person who doesn't panic under pressure who wins. It took me three seasons in athletics to learn that. I just used to come to meetings and run hard to win. But at the top level you can't just run hard and win. It's like driving a car with your eyes closed. After the first full three years all of a sudden I opened my eyes.'

TRAINING TO THRIVE UNDER PRESSURE

When under pressure, champions manage to keep thinking clearly and correctly. They are able to make the right decisions, regardless of the intense stress they are under. As Dr Ceri Evans from Gazing Performance Limited says, it is clear thinking that drives effective action; ineffective thinking leads to ineffective action. Anybody can think clearly in moments when they are under control, but it's thinking clearly under pressure that is difficult.

Whether seeking to maintain skill levels or to think clearly under pressure, there is no substitute for training.

Dr Ceri Evans and his colleagues at Gazing Performance advocate building in pressure situations to the skills acquisition and training process. In Gazing's recommended skills ladder, the first level of training should be focused on mastering the technical aspects of the skill, which often involves breaking it down into its component parts. Level two involves rehearsal of the skill with some intensity and pressure, indicative of playing or competing conditions. Level three of the training introduces diversions. Dr Evans says:

'To be successful under pressure you have to have experienced conditioning at all skill levels. Mental conditioning conducted solely in classroom-type settings is likely to have limited effect. It is better when it is integrated with the techni-

*cal and the physical. Players need conditioning to keep their
attention focused on the task.'*

Dr Evans gives an example of a player practising a throw to a
line-out in rugby. The skill components would include technical aspects such as how to stand and how to hold the ball,
while the whole technique involves the whole throwing action.
Intensity can be introduced by repetition, rehearsal when
physically stressed, and by using opposed lineouts. Pressure
can be introduced in various ways. Evans says:

> *'Before handing over the ball you could dunk it in water.
> You can distract the player with unexpected noise. The play-
> er's goal is to stay on task and not get diverted – stay with the
> rituals they have put in place.'*

Players need to practise maintaining their process focus during
real training sessions. These enable them to experience what
Gazing calls 'world lessons'. In contrast, learning something
in a classroom is more a 'word lesson' and not as powerful a
learning experience.

Evans gives the example of a karate drill. A young practitioner may start out learning and practising some hand
combinations. They may have been told to keep their hands
up to protect themselves and to maintain awareness for the
opponents' attacks, but how well do they learn the lesson? Dr
Evans says:

> *'As a trainer you could get them doing some combinations,
> and when they let their guard drift down the trainer can
> counterattack with the focus mitt. That focuses their atten-
> tion on keeping their hands up and defending themselves.
> If they drop their hands again the trainer can attempt to
> counterattack with the focus mitt again. Once they've got
> that idea, the trainer could unexpectedly attack with a leg
> kick. The student may drop their hands in surprise, thinking*

that they weren't warned about this possibility for the drill. Their response may let the trainer attack the exposed head again. Then they may finally understand what is meant by the concept of deliberately placing their attention on certain important tasks, and maintaining this focus in the face of predictable and unpredictable diversions. This can induce a heightened sense of awareness and improved control of attention. That might give them a "world" lesson, one they have experienced for themselves.'

Dr Stephanie Cook practised techniques for dealing with anxiety, such as breathing and relaxation techniques. She and her coach tried to recreate a sense of pressure in practice. She says:

'In shooting you want to be very calm and controlled and have a very steady hand. In a competition environment you have to deal with the affects of adrenalin, which causes a real physiological response. You have to know what to expect and then know how to deal with it. So when I was training we tried to simulate the competitive environment – we would have regular competitions so that I could train in ways to deal with competitive situations.'

Former England rugby head coach Clive Woodward and his coaching team tried to up the pressure during training sessions to see how players react.

'You want to try and create pressure situations. When it happens for real, you want the players to react positively. There are all sorts of ways you can try to create these pressure situations in training. The idea is that when it comes for real they will have rehearsed for it mentally. They've handled it and it should become a lot easier. So you can coach for coping with pressure, though I do believe a lot of it is innate. It's in there somewhere.'

AUTOMATIC PILOT

If players are to perform well under pressure they need to be able to switch into an 'automatic pilot' mode. They need to be able to function without having to think consciously about what they are doing.

Athletics coach Ron Roddan would train his athletes to run on automatic pilot. He would tell them how to run the 200 metres, how to start, run the bend and come off the bend. Every time they would get told the same thing. When they came to run an actual 200m race, Roddan would tell them to do what they did in training. In effect, he says, he basically brainwashed them. He told them what to do in training and then they didn't need to think about it in the race. As Roddan describes it, 'You have programmed the computer'.

It is important to be able to perform on automatic pilot right from the start of a race. Roddan says:

> *'Once the race starts it's a matter of making sure everything you have practised comes in automatically. Once the gun goes, your aim is just to get to the finish as quickly as possible. That's all you think about. You concentrate on one thing: move on the B of the Bang. That's the only thing you think about.'*

England rugby fly-half Jonny Wilkinson, when kicking for goal, relies on all the work he has done in training to put him on autopilot. He goes into his kick routine, a procedure he has rehearsed over and over again.

> *'As soon as you know you are going to kick you fall into that routine, which more or less shuts you off from everything. So I would set the ball up, move back a certain number of steps, check everything is in line, do a visualization of the path of the ball – where it's going to go and where I want it to go. Then I move to the side so I am now ready to kick. The routine then continues in a visualizing kind of way, but it's actually more of a sensation; I imagine the feeling I have*

when the ball hits the foot, the perfect feeling of how I want it to feel when it hits my foot, where I want it to hit my foot – what it's going to feel like when it goes right.

'Then I find a tiny dot dead centre between the posts, or wherever I am aiming. I visualize the line of the ball to that dot, as if the ball were on a wire attached to it. Then I have a kind of "centring" response, whereby I visualize all the power going from my central point down to where it needs to be, down my left leg and exploding from my left foot. I really feel that sensation. Then I really focus on the exact point on the ball I am going to hit and the part of my foot that I want it to come off. Then I send the ball up that wire.

'So I don't stand by the ball and say, "I am going to kick this, I feel fantastic". It's that as soon as I am given the kick I go into the routine I have done a hundred times a week in practice.'

Wilkinson has an unusual hand movement but this, he says, is just what happens to him when he is imagining all the power and the energy coming from the central point down to his leg. Similarly with the way he bends his knee – that's just the shape he finds himself in when thinking through the kick in advance. As Wilkinson says, the movement is a by-product of what is really important – which is him feeling strong and powerful and confident in what he is about to do.

Going through this routine also gives Wilkinson a sense of protection, despite the huge numbers of people watching.

'It's a very individual thing, and you are very much on your own out there when you are doing it. It's the way it has to be for me to be engrossed in what I am doing and shut off from everyone else and what they are doing. It allows me to get on with something I really need to succeed in. It makes me feel a bit protected and secure in the routine.'

Former Australian fly-half Michael Lynagh also relied on his automatic kicking routine in a pressure situation. He recalls a penalty awarded to Australia against England in the 1991 World Cup at Twickenham. Lynagh describes himself as going into 'an almost dazed state'. He says:

> *'I focused and concentrated on the routine – down to how I kneeled, how I would place the ball, the line I would see from the seam of the ball through to the middle of the posts. I wasn't thinking about the crowd because I was thinking about the task at hand.*
>
> *'Focusing on the outcome often causes failure. Focus on the task at hand and the outcome will look after itself.'*

THE PRESSURE OF PENALTIES

One of the most pressured situations in sport has to be the penalty shoot-out. As England football manager Sven Göran-Eriksson says:

> *'The walk from the middle circle to the penalty spot is a long walk, incredibly long. How many thoughts do you have during it?'*

The only way to succeed at penalty taking and deal with the intense pressure is to have developed a secure penalty-taking routine. Eriksson says:

> *'You must be focused. You must know exactly what you want to do. Don't let the opposition goalkeeper play tricks on you. It's a war with the goalkeeper, and he will do everything to try to disturb you.*
>
> *'Don't go to the spot early. Wait until the goalkeeper is more or less where he will be. Put the ball right on the spot. Don't try to cheat because then the referee will come and disturb you. Be sure where you want to put that penalty, and then do it, whatever happens.'*

The penalty-taking routine starts when the penalty takers enter the centre circle. It involves who players stand next to, what they do while they wait, what they think about and what the trigger is that gets them absolutely focused when it's their turn. Howard Wilkinson, former Football Association technical director, says:

'Do you leave the centre circle when the goalkeeper's got the ball, or when the referee's got the ball, or when the ball boy has got it? If you leave the centre circle when the goalkeeper or the ball boy's got the ball, you're not in charge; they are. If you go when the referee's got the ball, then you're in charge.'

The combination of good technique and strong mental approach makes a good penalty taker. Wilkinson believes that Alan Shearer has always inspired confidence when he steps up to take a penalty because he has both attributes. Wilkinson says that Shearer is not aware of his opponents or the crowd. He has no sense of anything else going on apart from his penalty kick. He just has the ability to focus entirely on the task in hand.

David Platt, former England captain, had a firm penalty routine. He recalls his attitude to taking penalties:

'I'd go to sleep the night before knowing what I'm going to do, having practised what I'm going to do, knowing where I am going to put that penalty. I would replay it in my mind. I could take the goalkeeper out of the equation because I knew that if I connected right and I put the ball where I wanted to put it, at the right velocity, then he wasn't going to get it anyway.

'Technique is important because everybody will have a negative thought. So you need the ability to block out those negative thoughts. I want to be in charge of the whole walk. I would never jog up – I think people do that because they are nervous. When people put a ball down and turn round, to me they're nervous. It's like they are turning away from the situation. But if that's their routine and what they're familiar with, then it's right and proper that they do it. But

for me, the fact that you're strolling out means you are slow-
ing it down because you're in control.

'There was one boy who took a penalty recently who I
thought really had some balls. He put the ball on the spot
and then he tied his bootlace before he took the penalty.
That is being in complete control of the situation.

'I believe I can trust my technique to score a goal and
I don't want anything else in my mind when I'm going up
from the halfway line to the penalty box. I know exactly
where I'm going to put the ball and I won't be changing my
mind. I made the mistake of changing my mind in 1990.'

PENALTY PRACTICE

With penalty taking, practice is vital. And the situation needs
to be as realistic as it can be, including trying to simulate the
distractions and the pressure. As England football manager
Sven Göran-Eriksson explains:

'You should try to be as prepared as possible. We practised
penalties during the World Cup and we told the goalkeeper
to try to distract the penalty takers. If they didn't put the ball
exactly on the spot, the referee – Ray Clemence – told them
to wait. It's difficult because you can never do it 100% real-
istically, because you can never put on the same pressure
during a practice. Imagine if you meet Argentina and go to
a penalty shoot-out. You are the last man up and you know
that if you score, you stay in the tournament, but if you don't
score, you go home.'

Trying to add pressure into the training practice can only help
players when it comes to the real thing. Eriksson believes that
even though you can't recreate the same pressure 100% perfectly, you can get part way. He says:

'In football practice you normally play seven against seven
or eight against eight for ten minutes. Instead of a team
having two corners, they have a penalty. Even though it's a

*practice, every player wants desperately to win that game.
They want desperately to win it.'*

Sports psychologist Professor Graham Jones believes it is
'absolutely crucial' to practise penalty taking. He considers
the requirements for successful penalty taking:

*'First of all you make a decision on where you're going
to put the ball, and then it's all process. If you've got any
doubts on where you're going to put the ball, stop. Be quite
certain. Don't just hit it as hard as you can.*

*'Once you know where you're going to put the ball, it's
process. You work through beforehand what you do. You
place the ball on the spot, walk back a certain number of
paces. Do you turn your back? Whatever you do, you do it
in the same way.*

*'The keeper will come out and try to distract penalty
takers, so they need to have worked through that as well.
They might think the keeper is doing it because he knows
they're going to score and therefore they should feel great
about it.*

*'It's about having complete control. The process is abso-
lutely crucial. It's the people who forget the process and try
to do things differently who get in a mess.'*

NLP trainer Graham Shaw has no doubt that there is plenty
that can be done to improve performance in penalty shoot-
outs. It is also possible to recreate the sense of pressure. Shaw
suggests how penalty practice could be built into training:

*'The first step would be to have the players go out and
practise kicking the ball into the net in exactly the way that
would be their ideal penalty shot. Then you could sit them
down and have them imagine that they're doing that every
single time. Then they go out and do it again for real. You
would probably have them keep a record so they can prove
it to themselves that it's working.'*

After that, you can develop strategies for dealing with the pressure of the real situation. Take a scenario where the final whistle has gone and the match is to be decided on penalties. Say that the sound of the final whistle, followed by the manager asking if you're ready to take a penalty, normally results in feelings of nerves and being scared. NLP can be used to identify those kinds of triggers and then develop a strategy for dealing with them.

For example, in this case the stimulus for the nervous response is the manager asking if you're ready to take a penalty. By putting something between the stimulus and the response, the performance can be improved. Without this, the nervous response can seem automatic. In fact, Shaw says, our responses are not all automatic; they just seem that way because we have done them so often. What we want is to have a choice about our response.

Shaw suggests getting players to practise their response, perhaps by having them waiting in the centre circle not knowing who is next up to take the penalty. This is where anchors, as referred to in Chapter 8, can be used to get players into the required state.

SELECTING THE PENALTY TAKERS

Sports psychologist Professor Graham Jones believes that choking during a penalty shoot-out is a sign of mental weakness. He says that mental toughness provides a barrier against choking, so choking is a function of not being mentally tough. Mentally tough people may have negative thoughts, but they get rid of them straight away, Professor Jones says. However, when people start to choke, when things are starting to go wrong, they lose some control of the environment. There's a snowball effect and things just get worse.

This means that when selecting players to take penalties, alongside basic technical ability there has to be mental toughness. Jones says:

'There has to be a combination of the two, but if selecting players, I would go with the people you think can handle the situation. They're not necessarily the people who step forward either, because a sign of mental weakness is actually stepping forward and thinking "I should be taking this, I'm expected to take this. I don't want to, but I'm going to." Mental weakness can be taken for mental toughness.'

There is no doubt that those who are chosen to take the penalties need to be happy to do so. England's players were asked if they were willing to take penalties before the World Cup. England football coach Sven Göran Eriksson says:

'First we talked about it and asked them if they wanted to take a penalty. Most of them wanted to. Then we practised.'

As this chapter has shown, champions understand the importance of training themselves to cope with pressure. They also understand the value of reviewing performances and learning from mistakes, a topic we turn to next.

Chapter 10

REVIEW AND REVISE

LEARNING FROM MISTAKES – and successes – is a key element of all top sporting champions' training routine. They review their performances and use that information to revise future training schedules or preparatory routines, all with a view to improving future performances.

REGULAR REVIEW

Sports psychologist Ian Lynagh says that after every performance athletes need to evaluate how they did. Then they need to review their goals. They might look at what they are doing well in their golf game – perhaps their drives are working well. However, they realize they need to work on their chipping and so they put that down for work during the week. Lynagh says that sportspeople might also review their emotional control, concentration, confidence, arousal control and so on – whatever the skills they want in their package. Lynagh says:

> *'A lot of athletes are encouraged to keep journals where they record their performances and their feelings at the time and learn from that. I would develop little ratings scales for athletes to rate themselves after a performance.*
>
> *'Athletes can only improve by being self-reflective. Athletes who don't do that can be on an emotional roller coaster. When they win they are euphoric and forget what made that possible; they don't learn from it. If they lose they get depressed and don't talk to anyone for days and again, they never learn anything.'*

Former national athletics coach Frank Dick believes that debriefing after an event is a matter of personal responsibility. Sportspeople have to 'take personal ownership' of the review process. Dick has worked with football club Ipswich Town's academy. He recalls how one particular lad had a moan one week after he had received 'a right bollocking'; he complained that no one said anything in the weeks they did well.

Dick is not impressed by such complaints, noting that a professional sportsman won't just sit back because the coach doesn't say anything.

> *'You should ask yourself, "Was I OK?". If you don't know the answer you should ask the coach. If the eleven people working together in the team got the right result, that's fine, but does that mean your performance was 100%? It may not. There may be something you should work on. You should score yourself out of ten for each aspect of your "game". Whether you've won, lost or drawn, you should be able to look yourself in the mirror and ask what you could do better next time. Winning is about being better today than you were yesterday. It's ridiculously arrogant that, having won, you walk away and don't look at your performance.'*

Dick believes that the debriefing should take place immediately after the event. As a coach, he knows that athletes will sometimes try and tell him what he wants to hear, rather than what they really think. The more time they have to compose themselves after an event, the better prepared their answers may be. But Dick doesn't want people to give him a cosmetic answer; a neat explanation in hindsight. He wants to know what they were really thinking or trying to do in the arena under pressure and that's more likely to happen sooner after the event than later. As Dick says, he wants to catch people when they are 'still expressive'.

Sprinter Mark Richardson also believes that a post-race review is invaluable, but he prefers to allow a little break before conducting it.

'I don't think you should do it straight after a race because it's the wrong time. If you've run badly, for example, you're too emotional. You need to come to terms with it first and analyse it with a logical mind, not an emotionally charged mind. Any post-race critique should happen a couple of days later. And if something went wrong, you talk it through with people who are close to you – your coach or manager.'

Olympic hurdler Sally Gunnell would have a relatively quick review of her performance in races in the run up to major competitions, but then move on to focus on the next race.

'My coach, Bruce Longden, would always find something good from a race. He might say, you could have done this at the seventh hurdle, but he always found something good and that gave me the confidence to move on.

'I don't think I ever ran the perfect race. Probably the nearest I got to it was in the World Championships in 1993, but there was probably a bit more I could do somewhere.

'I was always very good at forgetting about the last race and moving on – even straight after the Olympics. You had to look at it, learn quickly and move on.'

Yachtsman Sir Chay Blyth sees the value in reviewing situations that occur in order to learn lessons from them. How that review is performed depends on the situation in question, he says.

'If it's a one man thing, you just sit down and make a few notes. If it's a team situation, you sit down together and say, "Right, what the hell did we do wrong here?" In the first Whitbread Around the World yacht race we had a specially designed boat and when we arrived at Cape Town we were third. We should have been first. We got the team round and looked at what had happened, so we could refocus and regroup.'

CONTROLLABLES

England rugby captain Lawrence Dallaglio notes that it is important to focus your review on factors that are within your control. He believes that too many people get worried about things they can't influence and can't control. As Dallaglio says, you only have a certain amount of energy and if you expend some of it on things that you can't directly affect, you're wasting something that you could channel in the right direction.

Hurdling Olympic gold medallist Sally Gunnell also recognized during her career that it was a waste of energy to worry about what the competition was doing. She concentrated on her own training and preparation. Gunnell says:

'Former Olympic gold medallist David Hemery taught me that there's nothing you can do about anybody else, so why even worry about it? That's what a lot of athletes do. They worry about the competition, but there's nothing you can do about that. It's important to accept you can only make a difference to yourself.'

MISTAKES HAPPEN

Champions see mistakes and setbacks as learning opportunities. England rugby captain Lawrence Dallaglio recognizes that sportspeople can face all kinds of setbacks – on and off the field, in social terms as well as in their performance.

> *'The key is to learn from your mistakes. If you have had a setback, normally it's as a result of a mistake that you have made or someone else has made or you have made jointly. The key to succeeding after a setback is knowing why you failed, accepting the failure – not necessarily publicly, although you might in certain situations – and then learning from that.'*

Even great champions can make bad mistakes during their careers. Olympic hurdler Sally Gunnell proved her champion's quality when she came back from disappointment in the European Championships in 1990.

> *'I was the fastest in Europe going into that race. I'd won all the races leading up to it and I guess I just got too confident. I got too blasé about it. I just thought I'd got to turn up, run it and win it, and I ended up fifth.*
>
> *'That was my first real setback. I was absolutely devastated. I went off the track and cried my eyes out for probably 24 hours. I felt it was the end of the world; it was going to finish my career. I couldn't work out where I'd gone wrong. Then my coach, Bruce Longden, sat down with me and said, "You can't pack it all in. You've got to work out where you went wrong." I learnt a lot from that. Whatever happens, you've got to accept it to a certain extent, but then work out what went wrong.*
>
> *'I realized that I'd missed a big chunk of training because I'd gone down to Auckland, New Zealand, for the Commonwealth Games in the preceding December and January. Once I had found the reason I realized I had to move on, and make sure it never happened again.'*

The next year, going into the World Championships in Tokyo in 1991, Gunnell was one of the favourites to win gold.

'I found myself in the lead going off the ninth hurdle, with one more to go. Then I made a massive mistake again. I stuttered into the last hurdle and the Russian athlete, Tatyana Ledovskaya, came charging past me. She went on to win and I came second. I threw that world championship gold medal away. I thought, "I can't make a massive mistake like that again."'

The two major disappointments in 1990 and 1991 made Gunnell reassess her support team.

'I realized I needed more help around me. I realized I couldn't do it all on my own. You need a team around you. So I found a nutritionist to tell me what to eat. I was eating pretty much rubbish at that time; it was like I was trying to put diesel into a Formula One car. So I needed a nutritionist to advise me what to eat to create energy so I could go out there and run 100%. I also needed a physio to help me prevent injuries, rather than waiting until I had those injuries and then getting one. If I got a niggle I went straight off and found him. And then I had my coach, Bruce Longden, who was running all my track sessions and feeding me information. I also had my husband [Jon Bigg], who was doing all the training sessions with me. So it was a big team.'

Gunnell also decided to make use of a sports psychologist.

'I made that mistake in the 1991 World Championships and I had to make sure it didn't happen again. That mistake happened because I wasn't mentally prepared. So I met David Hemery, the 1968 Olympic gold medallist. He asked me how often I visualized before a race. I told him I sat down and did it the night before. He told me I couldn't be an Olympic champion like that; that you literally had to visualize it a year beforehand. This is where the difference is probably made between getting silver and gold medals.'

For more on Hemery's visualization advice, see Chapter 7.

Sebastian Coe looks back at the Moscow Olympics and his two finals – one a disaster, the other a triumph. Coe says that in the 800m he learnt how not to behave 20 minutes before an Olympic final, and in the 1500m he learnt the right way to do it.

On paper Coe was two seconds faster than anyone else in the 800m and was the world record holder. The expectation was that Coe would win the 800m final and Steve Ovett would win the 1500m. However, things didn't go to plan in the 800m. Coe describes it as 'an appalling race' and he finished second. His father, who was also Coe's coach, wasn't best pleased.

'He said he felt ashamed for himself because he had a major contribution in it. He is a fairly brutal, honest bloke. We had not spent ten years working two or three times a day from the age of fourteen onwards on windswept Yorkshire moors and rainswept tracks for me to run as badly as I did.'

The newspapers wrote critically about Coe's performance, but this acted as a spur for the 1500m. He received the UK Sunday papers in the Olympic village three days late. The front page of the *News of the World* displayed a photo of him on his training run the day after the 800m with 'Coe's trail of shame' written underneath. The criticism increased his motivation to come back with a win in the 1500m.

Mary Peters, the team manager, also helped to inspire Coe.

'Mary was great. I knew her really well and she was quite tough about it. She said, "You have run an appalling race. There is no point telling you that because you know it. You are lucky because if you had been another athlete – such as Jim Ryan, the American world record holder who was tripped up in 1972 by an unseeded African competitor – your Olympic career would be over. But you can get back onto that track in four days' time and go out and win another title. You don't have to wait four years to do it." She was quite right.'

When it came to the 1500m final Coe was psyched up for the task. He describes himself as in the best shape of his life and knowing that he had to win it. Happily for Coe, he did. The gold was his.

One other race that didn't go too well for Coe – one that he looks back on as the most important race of his career – took place in the 800m in Prague. Coe came third, but he feels that he learnt a huge amount from the experience.

> *'A great fallacy in sport and other walks of life is that people think it's only when you win that you succeed. They think failure is automatically linked with losing, and it's not. I learnt more in finishing third in that one race than I learnt in the ten or twelve years leading up to it. In the 800m in Prague I was running against Steve Ovett for the first time in my career. I decided the only way I could beat him was to try and run the legs off him from the front, because I wasn't quick enough at that time in my career to outkick him.*
>
> *'I ran the first lap faster than anyone had ever done in an 800 metres. I got to 600m feeling quite good and then I got to 610m and I thought the world was caving in. I remember Steve came past me in the finishing straight and then to his complete shock an East German came past both of us.*
>
> *'I then realized two things. First of all, you never ever go into a race thinking about just one competitor; you recognize there is a race and there are other people capable of doing things. You have to think about the whole field. Secondly, most people said I was mad to have gone through the first lap in the time I did, but I probably would not have got a medal if I hadn't gone at that pace. The one thing I knew was that I had one year, two at the most, to get myself in training to not only go through the first lap slightly quicker, but then to hold on for a second lap. That is exactly what I did in the winter of 1979.*
>
> *'I completely changed my approach to the distance work I was doing and the kind of speed and endurance work I was doing on the track. I broke the world record nine months*

later. So if you ask me what was the foundation stone of my career, it was that race in Prague.'

SUCCESS MATTERS

It isn't just poor performances that provide good learning material. Former national athletics coach Frank Dick believes it essential to review your winning performances too. He believes that it is as important to know why you have won as it is to know why you haven't. As he says: 'If you don't know why you won, it was an accident.'

Professor Graham Jones agrees that analysing success can give valuable insights for a sportsperson. He says that people tend to forget the things that have gone well. Instead they focus on what has gone wrong. Professor Jones says that his approach has always been to build on what's going well – to understand why someone is doing really well at something. After Wales beat France in Paris in the 2001 Six Nations, Professor Jones advised Graham Henry, the Welsh coach, to spend a session before the next game on working out what was great about the match. He says:

'The players split up into small groups and worked out what was good and what they needed to make happen again. Then they could work on things they needed to do to build on it, rather than things that weren't good. For me, it's crucial that you build your foundation from what's good and you revisit your successes every single time.'

Mark Richardson, 400m Commonwealth silver medallist, also notes that there is value in reviewing why a race has gone well: he says he is always aware of what made a race successful. He doesn't believe you need to go into as much detail in the analysis, but stresses that it is important to recognize why you performed well. As he says, if you don't, how on earth are you going to recreate that performance at a later date?

OPEN TO INNOVATION

An important aspect of the review and revise process that champions use is their willingness to try new things. You might look at what went wrong, for example, but unless you can come up with a solution or a new approach to try, you can't do better next time.

Former badminton champion Gill Clark believes that 'being an innovator' is one of the undersung characteristics of a champion. She was always looking for new techniques that she could use in preparing to take on her badminton opponents.

'Champions are always looking to do it a bit better, which means not necessarily using the same training methods that everybody else has used. How can we do it a little bit differently? What is it that means I can get the edge over somebody else?'

In some sports the only way to make it to the top is as a result of some kind of quantum leap – a complete, radical revision to how things are done. This is the case in motorsport, as Ron Dennis, boss of the McLaren racing team, explains. Motorsport requires a particular approach when a racing team is not doing as well as it might and trying to get back on top. Dennis says:

'Motorsport is different from other sports where the sporting equipment has generally remained unchanged for years. In motorsport, you get dramatic change. So to go back and look at what you did two years ago is immaterial. You can learn from the past, but Formula One doesn't respond well to this sort of systematic approach. If you are successful, as Ferrari have been, then you are only making incremental changes.

'The only way to catch them is to make a quantum leap, for example, by changing supplier or radically redesigning

*the chassis or engine. You have to be entrepreneurial in the
way you make progress.'*

Experimentation and being willing to try new things is important for achieving success in all walks of life, not just sport.
The ability to adapt increases our potential not only to record
one-off winning performances, but also to repeat our success
time and again.

In training themselves to achieve repeated success, sporting champions often call on coaches to give them advice and
support. We examine the nature of the relationship between
sportsperson and coach in the next chapter.

Chapter 11

COACHING RELATIONSHIPS

BEHIND EVERY GREAT SPORTING CHAMPION there is often a great coach. That coach may or may not have worked with the athlete throughout their career. However, successful coaches always have the qualities the elite sportspeople need to perform at their peak on a consistent basis.

COACH SUPPORT

Clive Woodward, former England rugby head coach, says that his role, and that of his support staff, was to give the England players every opportunity to achieve, win matches and be the best in the world.

Woodward knows that success on the field requires the right supporting environment off the field.

> *'I've never seen things going right on the pitch unless they're going right off it. When I walked into the England coach role there was nothing going right off the field. I had to change everyone's thinking in terms of how we were going to operate and how to be a high performance team. I got involved in getting the environment right.'*

England football manager Sven-Göran Eriksson also believes that coaches need to create supportive environments that encourage footballers to try new things, without worrying about the repercussions of making mistakes. This is part and parcel of daring to win – taking appropriate risks that make winning possible.

> *'I am not a psychologist, but I try to use what I have learned: be calm, be positive and give courage to your players.*
>
> *'If you are a winger, you have to try to beat the fullback. The risk is that you may lose the ball. Okay, we take that risk, because if you never try, you will never beat the opposition.*
>
> *'Sometimes you have players who are afraid of making mistakes. But if you are afraid of making mistakes, you will never try something difficult. You don't want the ball. You're hiding. You never try to dribble, or to make a cross, or to try a shot on goal. You have to give players courage so that they aren't afraid to fail. As a coach, if you start shouting at the player who gives a bad pass, then you take him down – you don't help him. A football player never goes out meaning to give a bad pass, or to do bad things. He always tries to do good things. So it's important as a leader that you don't start shouting once he makes mistakes.*
>
> *'You must always be positive and never lose your temper. If a player has failed, makes a mistake, forget it and try to be positive.*

> *'The player must feel secure. You defend the player against the press, directors, friends or whoever.*
>
> *'Of course, if the player always makes the same mistake, then you have to tell them they can't do it every time. You can't risk doing difficult things in the midfield because you create problems for the whole team. If someone does stupid things five or ten times in every game, then you have to show it's not acceptable.'*

Sometimes Eriksson's wisdom alone has not been sufficient to give a player the courage to take the necessary risks – the courage to risk making a mistake. In such situations he calls on the services of a sports psychologist.

> *'For example, one of the players I had in Italy was afraid. He was a centre forward and extremely good, but during the big games he was afraid of failure, afraid to be kicked. I worked with him for one year and he didn't improve. I recognized that I couldn't help him any more. So I took him to see Willi Railo [a leading sports psychologist] and after six months he was the best centre forward in Europe. He became a great, great player thanks to Willi's involvement.'*

Of course, a coach cannot make an athlete or sportsperson believe in themselves if the individual doesn't have an inner core of self-belief already. Former sprinter and coach John Regis says belief has to start with the athlete, but is then reinforced by the coach:

> *'It comes initially from the athlete. The individual has to believe that they can – they have to believe that their talent and ability and mindset can get them where they want to be. Then the coach manipulates that so the athlete can call on their belief to get the best performance at a particular point. It's about the individual having the courage to believe in themselves, and the coach reinforcing that, saying "yes you can, you are good enough, you've done the training".'*

QUALITIES IN THE COACH

If a coach is to be able to bring out the best in talented sportspeople, then the coach requires certain characteristics and qualities. What does it take to be a good coach or manager?

Sven-Göran Eriksson believes that for a manager to be successful, he has to be true to himself.

'As a boss, as a leader, you have to be yourself. You can't go and play another role. The Italy manager Giovanni Trapattoni's style on the bench is fantastic to see. It's worth the ticket. His whistling is fantastic. That's his style. But I can't do that because I would feel stupid. I have to be myself in front of the players. As a player you want your manager to be genuine, in whatever way that is.

'I always keep a certain distance from the players, and I don't know if that's good or not. But I never thought a football player would want to go out eating with his manager. I don't think he's comfortable doing that. You need to keep a certain distance, but on the other hand, players should never be afraid of coming to you with a problem they have, whether it's on the field or off the field. And I'm always happy when a player comes to me saying, "Boss, do you think we could do this in another way?" Then you know you have involved them. I never thought I knew everything about football, so if players come to me with opinions, that's excellent. As a coach you have to ask what players think, because if they get involved, they will play much better.'

Former sprinter John Regis tries to pass on the benefit of his experiences to the athletes he coaches, but he accepts that they sometimes need to learn some things for themselves. Even so, being given a suggestion about how to look at a problem or tackle an issue can help young athletes to get over whatever it is more quickly. That means they can perform at the desired, high level more quickly or more consistently.

Regis believes that coaches need to speak to athletes in plain and simple terms, rather than making what they say too technical.

> 'The athlete has to understand what you are saying and have belief in what you are saying. I'm fortunate because I've been there, done that and got the T-shirt. So I can demonstrate what I'm looking for and the athlete can see it vividly. Then he can absorb that and adapt it to his technique.'

Adrian Moorhouse had a long-standing relationship with one particular coach – Terry Denison. Denison expected Moorhouse not only to train, but also to learn about physiology so that he understood the body's system. Then they could have a proper dialogue about the training. Moorhouse says:

> 'Terry didn't just want me swimming up and down, he wanted intelligent talking feedback – a protégé if you like. The more I knew about physiology, the more we had conversations.'

RELATIONSHIP DEVELOPMENT

Former national athletics coach Frank Dick believes that the relationship between sportsperson and coach develops over time.

> 'As a young athlete you start off accepting. You get told by your coach, "this is what you do". Then after a while you start having the courage to ask questions and exploring. That's your curiosity coming through. You shift from being an "acceptor" to an "explorer". Then, once you start to explore enough, the bit of drive and ambition in you encourages you to challenge. You develop self-confidence and you become a "challenger". Once you feel really strongly about it you want to be a "winner". Once you've won a couple of times you want to be remembered forever because of your quality of winning and you try to become a "champion".'

Those who go on to become legends in their sports don't stop at simply becoming a champion, Dick believes. They are driven to achieve real greatness. Those people have a level of self-belief that they continue to contribute towards a greater dynasty.

Champions' single-minded determination means they aren't afraid to challenge their coaches, Dick says. Their sense of self-belief and single-mindedness can lead them to feel they need to know all there is to know about what they are doing. Therefore, challenging the coach is a natural thing to do. Dick says that he was quite comfortable with Olympic decathlete Daley Thompson, Boris Becker (tennis), Katarina Witt (skating), Gerhard Berger (Formula One), Ronnie Irani (cricket), Justin Rose (golf), and other top performers, challenging him on almost every programme they worked on together.

Sports psychologist John Syer also believes the relationship between a coach and the athlete should change over time.

> *'The athlete certainly needs technical coaching and it is primarily up to the coach to establish a productive relationship. However, success depends on the initial relationship developing into that of a two-person high performing team. This means reaching the stage where they are able to challenge each other. When challenges are well expressed and well timed, they allow the relationship's potential to emerge, as together they find new ways of doing things that neither of them might have discovered alone. Eventually, the athlete may need new input and the coach may also feel it is time to move on.'*

The relationship that former sprinter John Regis had with his coaches developed as he became more experienced. He also changed coaches when he felt he had learnt all he could from them.

> *'Once I'd got all the information I could from a coach, I felt we reached a plateau. We were both at the same level. So I would move to somebody who had more informa-*

tion. I always needed someone there I could look at, who would give me the information I required. When you're good enough you know technically what you're doing, but for things like block starts you still do need a coach. You try so hard to generate power and speed that you may do something wrong that may need tidying up. I had about six coaches in my career. I needed somebody who was keeping me on my toes, who knew more than me.'

When advising young sprinters, Regis gives them a chance to identify areas for improvement. After a competition they sit down together and go through what happened. Regis gives the athlete a chance to give his own analysis of what he did right and what he did wrong. With top athletes, 95 times out of 100 they come up with the correct analysis, Regis says. This comes in part from the athlete's knowledge of their own body. Regis notes that top athletes know their own bodies inside out. They also know great technique from poor technique, whether in terms of arm action or knee lift. As Regis says, a good athlete should in each stride know what they're doing.

Before a race Regis doesn't give a pep talk as such. He explains:

'I just listen. I say, "Go and do what you do best. You've trained for it, so just go and do it." At the end of the day the athlete holds his career in his own hands – or in his own feet.'

In general, sportspeople need to be independent-minded to be successful. Michael Lynagh, former Australian rugby captain and renowned fly-half, feels he was 'very lucky' with his coaches.

'I became very close to most of them and worked closely with them. Some would say I was very pig-headed and hard to change, which I would probably agree with, but I would always talk to the coaches. I would never just say they were

wrong and not talk to them. I would explain why I thought what I did.

'I had certain ideas of how I operated on the pitch and that might have been pretty intimidating for some coaches and players. But I thought I was always pretty fair and my sole goal was to get the team to perform better and to win. I thought my motives were right.'

Former badminton champion Gill Clark believes that as sport has become more professional, so full-time coaches are taking too much control.

'They are arranging travel, telling the athletes what time to practise, setting up their training programmes on a daily basis. The athlete is becoming a zombie. But the ones who are really successful think for themselves. Michael Johnson is absolutely spot-on. He thinks for himself, and that's why he's been so successful.

'Players need to be encouraged and taught to take personal responsibility. The coach is there to help, but you know the old expression – you can lead a horse to water but you can't make it drink. I could tell a player what to do, but they're the ones who have to go out and do it. They've got to perform, and if they've got to perform, they've got to believe 102% that what they're doing is correct, instead of just thinking the coach told them to do it.'

QUALITIES IN A GOOD RELATIONSHIP

Sports psychologist and former national volleyball coach John Syer believes that a successful coaching relationship requires certain qualities. He says there must be respect, trust and the opportunity for each of the people involved to discover things they didn't know. As Syer says, this is only achieved when those concerned are self-aware, aware of each other and able to appreciate their differences.

Sports psychologist and performance specialist Professor Graham Jones has a similar view, that having trust and confidence in one another is key to the coach–player relationship. It's got to be reciprocal. Nobody knows an athlete better than the athlete himself or herself. Professor Jones says that when you talk about the world's top performers, they know themselves much better than anybody else and so the coach almost has to fit in with them.

> 'The coach plays a key role in helping to build performance self-belief, the ability to handle pressure and so on. The performers then have to take that on board.
>
> 'I believe that coaches empower athletes, yet I still come across coaches at a very senior level who take a very transactional approach in terms of "This is the way it's going to be". In this day and age you don't get many of those coaches working with the world's best, because the best in the world know what they want, they know what's best for them. At that top level the coach almost becomes a mentor rather than a coach, and that's a very different relationship.'

Former England Under-21 coach, David Platt, recalls being impressed by former England manager Graham Taylor's ability to inspire trust and belief in his players. Taylor, he says, was able to speak to players in a manner that was respectful, whether one-on-one or in groups. He put pressure on players, but they always felt he was on their side. Platt says that Taylor got into his psyche. He delivered his words in a manner that meant he and the other players actually believed what he was saying.

> 'For me, too, I have to portray to my players that I believe they can win, that it's not just words. That's what Graham could do. The way he spoke, you thought it wasn't just words – he actually believed it.
>
> 'Sven also gets the players to believe that he's with them and he trusts them. He puts great trust in his players. He doesn't ask them to do things; he puts them under pressure to perform. When he speaks to them he demands things of them in a respectful way, but he believes in them.'

At Nottingham Forest, Platt worked hard to understand his players.

> *'I had different characters at Forest. By the end of a two-year period I could influence the players I had in the club. I knew what made them tick and I could make them tick. It might be knocking them down or picking them up. It might be handling them respectfully, it might be tolerating their deficiencies without embarrassing them. Everybody has got a different character and as a manager you can't treat everybody in the same manner. You have to find out what makes the player tick and then you treat the player in the way that means you can get the best out of him.'*

From the age of 15 onwards, Sally Gunnell had the same coach throughout her career – Bruce Longden, who was also the coach of Daley Thompson. Gunnell feels that having the same coach gave her extra stability. By the peak of her career, the relationship between Gunnell and Longden had naturally matured, but still retained essential characteristics of trust and belief. By the top of her career Gunnell had amassed a wealth of personal knowledge, but she still found she needed Longden to be there. She needed him to be 'saying the right things' and she needed to believe in what he said. As Gunnell remarks:

> *'A lot of coaching relationships go wrong because the athletes end up not believing what the coach says. With Bruce, I always knew that every single training session he set me was right and that it would make a difference. He planned every session. I would do it and he would watch me and time me. And as long as you believe that you're doing the right thing, you're halfway there.*
>
> *'If I had run a bad race, Bruce would find a reason why, and he was right. That was fine because then I could move on. I believed everything he said. He was quite a hard coach and a lot of people couldn't get on with him. But I guess it's hard training people and he expected a lot of an athlete.'*

A TOUCH OF TOUGHNESS

Whatever the duration of the coaching relationship, whether at the start or many years down the training line, coaches do need to be prepared to be tough in their athletes' own interests. Former national athletics coach Frank Dick was prepared to be tough with athletes who didn't commit wholeheartedly to their training regime and who didn't understand that training was directly linked to performance in competition.

> 'You've got to make a commitment. That means every time you train, everything you do is in line with the objective you're going for. I remember falling out with an athlete I was working with in preparation for the AAA Championships. We'd agreed the squad was going to be out there training every night of the week. On the Monday night the squad was all ready to go except this athlete, who turned up a bit late. He got a bollocking for that. Then he said he'd forgotten his shorts. So I wouldn't let him train.
>
> 'Every time you train it's a rehearsal. It has to demonstrate the unshakeability of what's going to happen in the arena. Learn to live with no second chances.'

Dick believes that training must always be conducted with the same attitude required for the day of competition. Giving your best and doing things the right way has to become instinctive. Champions understand the importance of such training. Every player, whether in football, athletics or any sport, has to know why they are going to training, Dick says. At the end of the training they should also know whether they achieved what they wanted, and what they have to work on next time.

Dick believes that coaches need to develop a strong, disciplined framework for the sportspeople they work with.

> 'You start off with your values. You've also got to agree your vision. And you make your journey towards that vision. Attitudes and behaviours are shaped out of that. It's because of the notion of personal discipline in your code of values that behaviours begin to shape.'

Analysis III

MENTAL TRAINING

THE BUILD-UP TO SPORTING COMPETITION is key to success under pressure on the day. In Part III we looked at the mental training processes and techniques sporting champions use to prepare themselves effectively.

CHAPTER 7

Many of the sporting champions we interviewed used visualization techniques to help them prepare for competition. In Chapter 7: Mental Rehearsal, we looked at how they practised visualization and how it helped them achieve their sporting goals.

Although people talk about visualization, the process is actually much more than simply visualizing yourself completing an action. Effective visualization involves recreating the sensations of the action – the feelings of running on the track, the sound of the crowd, or the other runners beside you. It draws in all aspects of the experience. It requires regular practice; it is a skill that needs to be learnt just like any other.

Visualization is a useful element of the sporting champion's armoury, when combined with training and skills acquisition. It can be used to reinforce the individual's physical talent and skills by enhancing their mental strength. However, it should not be seen as the single route to delivering world-beating performances. Without talent and skills already being in place, the value of visualization alone is limited. As Ceri Evans from mental conditioning specialists Gazing Performance says, visualization is potentially useful but it is not an answer for everything, nor is it enough on its own. You can't just lie down on a couch and imagine things and expect they will all just happen for you. They are not going to happen if you haven't got the necessary skill base, the skill acquisition framework and the confidence derived from gradually acquiring competence.

Sporting champions use visualization techniques to experience in their minds a perfect performance, with the aim of being able to recreate this perfect performance in the heat of competition. The individual needs to feel totally involved in the experience – seeing the things they would see in a race, hearing the same sounds, smelling the same smells.

The technique can also be used to re-edit a past experience so as to dampen its impact on the individual. This can be helpful if an athlete made a mistake in competition and then keeps reliving that experience in the mind. Re-editing the visualization so that it ends positively can reduce the chance of the athlete making the same mistake again – because the mind is reprogrammed to expect a different outcome. Renzie Hanham from Gazing Performance says that when people have had a bad performance they often replay it in their head in a way that retraumatizes them. Visualization can help because if people change the way they run through the experience in their heads, the impact is diminished.

Visualization can also be helpful in encouraging individuals to feel more at home in a strange environment.

When preparing for a competition, visualization can also be useful as a form of scenario planning. The individual can consider different situations that could arise and then visualize themselves dealing with them successfully. This can encourage the feeling of confidence before a performance, because the individual believes that every eventuality has been considered and that they are prepared to deal with anything that happens.

As Renzie Hanham points out, there is a difference between expectation and anticipation. When people expect something to take place, the implication is that the future is carved in stone. This approach doesn't allow for the unexpected and makes adaptation difficult; it can lead to denial – 'this can't be happening'. Anticipating what might happen allows for flexibility in the way we respond to a situation. We adapt, deal with it and then get back on track.

Applications

- Think of a positive experience that you have had where you did well, and that you want to recreate. To visualize the experience again, make sure you are sitting comfortably and are relaxed. Close your eyes and put yourself back into the experience. Try to see it through your own eyes, rather than seeing yourself as if you were watching a film of yourself. What did you hear at the time? Were there any smells you remember? Go through the experience in your mind from start to finish. How strongly were you able to recreate the experience? Do you feel more positive about being able to recreate it? Think about whether there are any more sensations you can introduce to enhance the experience. For example, how did the wind feel on your face? Was the racquet rough or smooth in your hand?
- You can use such visualizations for scenario planning. Think about things that could happen unexpectedly during the experience you are recreating. What if someone starts

heckling you during your speech? What if your slide pro-
jector breaks down? Before starting the visualization come
up with some solutions for how you could deal with such
situations effectively and successfully. When you have the
solutions, go through the visualization, but include the
unexpected situation and your successful reaction to it.
Make sure that the end is a positive one where you come
out on top. At the end you should feel increased confidence
in your ability to deal with such situations if they arise.

• There may be a past event which bothers you and where
you would like to diminish the impact that the memory of it
has on you. Perhaps you were in a situation where you felt
humiliated. You may be able to reduce the impact of the
memory by using certain techniques that create a sense of
distance between you and the memory. For example, when
you recall the past event, imagine you are seeing it played
out on a cinema screen. See yourself sitting in a chair in
front of the screen watching the drama unfold – with you as
one of the 'actors'. In this way you have removed yourself
somewhat from the direct action. See the event played in
black and white. (Colour tends to make experiences more
vivid.) Now try giving the characters silly, high-pitched car-
toon voices. You might add in the sound of a honky tonk
piano for added comic effect. Perhaps you could give some
of the characters huge mouse ears. Play around with the
images. You can speed the film up and run it backwards.
If you can make yourself laugh at the screen, the negative
impact of the memory should be hugely reduced; if the
memory comes to mind, the chances are it will trigger a
humorous association rather than the negative emotions of
before.

CHAPTER 8

In Chapter 8: Anchors and Triggers, we looked at how sporting champions can use techniques to recreate desired mental
states at will. We looked at how Neuro-Linguistic Programming
(NLP) can be used to programme your mind for success.

Useful techniques for this include anchors and triggers. Athletes can anchor feelings of confidence that they have experienced in the past and use triggers to experience them again at will. Anchors can take many different forms, such as images, sounds or even pieces of clothing. Olympic swimmer Adrian Moorhouse even used the pain he felt during a race as a trigger to release a surge of adrenalin. When modern pentathlete Dr Stephanie Cook pulled down her mask before a fencing match, that was her trigger to create the mental state she needed to fence well.

The experiences of our champions and experts show that anchors and triggers are useful tools to help maintain an individual's focus on the processes required for their sport, rather than becoming distracted by other things – the crowd, their nerves or other competitors. They can also be of use in everyday life, to help us maintain our attention on what we are doing.

Renzie Hanham from mental conditioning specialists Gazing Performance describes anchors and triggers as 'useful parts of the sportsperson's toolbox'. They enable individuals to put their attention where it is going to be most useful. This can be particularly valuable for specific situations, such as kicking in rugby, enabling attention to be focused on the current process that really matters.

If such anchors and triggers are to be effective, they need to be practised regularly and used in training as well as in the heat of competition.

Applications

- Think of a mental state you would like to be able to recreate at will. For example, perhaps you want to be able to maintain a sense of calm even in situations you find stressful, such as visiting the dentist. The basic way to do this is to relax in an environment where you feel comfortable and think back to an occasion where you felt this sense of calm. Perhaps it was when you were floating in the Mediterranean sea on your last holiday. Maybe it was when you were planting out spring bulbs in the garden. Recreate that experience by reliving it in your mind. See with your eyes the things you saw then. Feel the same sensations. Bring the experience vividly to life. Try making the images larger and brighter and see whether that makes the sensation of calm even more powerful.

- When you feel absolutely calm and fully involved in the sensation, the next step is to anchor it to a particular part of your body. For example, you might squeeze the tip of the little finger on your left hand. In this way you create a link between the feeling of that squeeze and a calm mental state.

- When you have squeezed your little finger once, return your focus to reliving the calm experience. Recall the sights, sounds and sensations again. Make them vivid and then once again, when you are fully reliving the experience, squeeze your little finger in the same place as before.

- By repeating this process several times you are reinforcing the link between the squeeze on your finger and the feeling of calm. This should mean that in future, if you find yourself getting worked up or anxious when you don't want to be, you can squeeze your little finger and trigger that feeling of calm.

- You can, of course, use the same technique to anchor a range of mental states, such as enthusiasm or determination. Just make sure that you use different triggers for each, i.e. don't anchor everything to the tip of your little finger! Ideal places are those that you can access easily but other people can't.

CHAPTER 9

In Chapter 9: Preparing for Pressure, we looked at how top sportspeople learn to handle the pressure that comes with top level competition, and even thrive on it.

Part of this involves simply accepting that competing at the highest level inevitably brings pressure. However, top athletes over time also develop the belief that they can handle that pressure because they have come through similar situations before.

Renzie Hanham from mental conditioning specialists Gazing Performance notes that the ability to function at an optimum level is often contextual. He says that an individual may be able to cope with stress in the sporting domain and yet not be able to deal with pressure in a relationship or in the workplace. This is partly because we have trained ourselves in one context and developed the necessary skills, but we haven't developed similar skills in another context. Our processes may not be as highly tuned in that other area because the context does not have sufficient significance for us to make the kind of effort required to perform at our best.

Our research amongst our sporting champions found that the key requirement for any champion is to be able to think correctly under pressure. This is what former England rugby head coach Clive Woodward looked for in his players. However, it isn't just a natural ability to think correctly under pressure that counts; champions learn how to do it and practise their skills in pressurized situations to do so. By trying to recreate the feeling of pressure that they experience on the pitch or on a running track, sporting champions become increasingly able to perform well regardless of the pressure they may feel.

Ceri Evans from Gazing Performance notes that top performers repeatedly drill themselves and practise their skills. They establish competence and then subject it to pressurized situations in training, perhaps by being subjected to a lot of noise or having to perform the skill when tired. They drill it so that they can remain focused on the process.

Some athletes and coaches, such as athletics coach Ron Roddan, describe this ability to perform regardless of the pressure as going into 'automatic pilot'. Athletes learn their skill or technique so well that they can produce it automatically – almost unconsciously – as needed. They 'over-learn' the skill; it becomes so embedded that they don't need to think about how to do it. England rugby hero Jonny Wilkinson, for example, has practised his kicking so thoroughly that when called on to kick in a game, he just automatically goes into his kicking routine.

Penalty taking, whether in rugby, football, hockey or any other sport, is one of the most high-pressure situations any sportsperson can experience. Yet some people love nothing better than to step up to the mark. Successful penalty takers are keen to put themselves and their reputations on the line, but they can't just rely on a gung-ho spirit. They practise their routine – from the moment they walk up to the spot – over and over again.

Some people may appear naturally good at coping with pressure, but that doesn't mean we can't all learn to do so. The first step is to frame the experience in a positive way. For example, if you can see pressure as exciting and stimulating rather than threatening, you are more likely to view it as a positive experience.

Most importantly, there is no replacement for practice. If you have to do something under pressure, you must practise it repeatedly. Once you have the basic skill and can perform under relaxed conditions, then you must increase the pressure little by little to reinforce that skill. You need to develop the ability to go into automatic pilot mode, regardless of what is going on around you.

Applications

- Is there some skill that you want to apply in a situation where you feel under pressure? Perhaps you are nervous of public speaking, but would like to be confident that you can do this well. One solution is to practise your skill in environments of steadily increasing pressure; start gently and build up gradually, increasing your confidence as you go.
- There is no substitute for rehearsal. Using the example of public speaking, start out by simply practising giving a talk in the privacy of your own home, where you are your only audience. Then try yourself out in front of someone you trust, such as a family member or friend. Make the most of any positive suggestions they make. If possible, take advan-

tage of any situations where you can talk in front of a small group of people – perhaps a group of colleagues at work. If you build up your confidence gradually, you will find that you are more comfortable with speaking in front or larger and larger audiences.

- Seize opportunities that come your way to practise your skills. Think of them as positive learning experiences that are helping you to develop in the ways that you want.
- Accept that you will probably always have some nerves when speaking in public – or doing anything else where your performance matters to you; virtually everyone does. In fact, those nerves can help to sharpen your performance.

CHAPTER 10

In Chapter 10: Review and Revise, we looked at how sporting champions review their performances and learn from their successes and their mistakes.

A regular review of performance is invaluable for checking that an athlete is on track in terms of their performance and outcome goals. Coaches clearly play an important role in giving feedback on what went well and what could be improved.

The timing of these reviews depends on the individual and the circumstances. Some people need a breathing space before they pick over their performance; their emotions may be running too high immediately after a competition to be able to think rationally about their performance. Some people prefer to look at the performance when it is still extremely fresh.

A key lesson that emerged from our champions was that the review should be focused on things the athlete can control. Worrying about what your competitors did is unhelpful.

Another key lesson is that mistakes can be learning opportunities. In a sense, there are no mistakes, only learning opportunities. Pretty much everyone slips up sometime, but the champions look for what they can learn from these experiences. Is there something they can do differently next time? Olympic hurdler Sally Gunnell suffered two major disappointments in 1990 and 1991, but moved on from the experiences by strengthening the support team she had around her.

Renzie Hanham from mental conditioning specialists Gazing Performance says that a useful way to perceive setbacks is to not think of them as failure, only feedback. It is more useful to think of a mistake as feedback, because feedback is useful information; it doesn't have the emotional response associated with the word 'mistake'. However, Hanham notes that feedback is often couched in negative terms such as 'Don't do this' or 'What do you think you were doing?', which is often inappropriate. Giving instructions in the negative implies the individual is doing something wrong and this can lead to an unhelpful emotional response, Hanham says. Feedback should be given as clear, specific instructions about what the individual can do. This allows the individual to stay focused on process and on improving the quality of the task. There are, however, occasions when giving instructions in the negative is useful, especially when individuals/teams find themselves mentally 'stuck'. Sometimes when people 'freeze', a sharp shout or comment can liberate them from this state and get them back into a meaningful process and on task. An example of this can be found in Zen: when trainees' attention starts to wane, the 'teacher' will utter a shout or strike them to 'unlock' them and get them back on task.

The key word here is 'trust' – between coach and athlete – and trust is something that is built up over time. Along with trust comes consistency of behaviour. That said, sometimes the unexpected comment or action can work to refocus the athlete, but if there is no trust then such interventions may be perceived as abusive and you can encounter resistance or withdrawal from the athlete.

Some of our interviewees, such as former England rugby coach Clive Woodward, believe that winning performances deserve even more review and analysis than losing performances. If you focus on what you have done right, you are more likely to be able to reproduce that winning performance again in future.

Being open to innovation was also a characteristic that many of our top sporting champions displayed. They were willing to consider new ideas and training techniques that could improve their performance in any possible way. Perhaps people in other areas of life could learn from sporting champions here. Renzie Hanham notes that people in the business world are generally less interested than sportspeople in psychological issues and learning about how mental conditioning can give them the edge. Business people tend to be more combative and less open to such ideas, perhaps because they don't feel particularly secure in the working environment.

Applications

- If there are areas of your life where you want to improve your performance, develop the habit of reviewing what you have done and how you did it. What was it about your performance that pleased you? Why did this go well? How can you try to ensure you do this similarly well in future? What aspects do you think you could have handled better? How could you try to improve these in future? Are there extra skills you can develop or existing ones you can improve?

  Try to conduct such reviews in a calm frame of mind. Don't perform them if you are feeling upset. Give yourself enough time that you can apply a slightly detached, rational approach, but don't leave it so long that you can't remember the details well enough.
- Consider seeking feedback from other people you respect. If you do, be prepared to give their comments a fair hearing and try not to react emotionally. See such feedback as a chance to learn and improve.

CHAPTER 11

Few top sportspeople achieve their success entirely on their own. All of them will have worked with a coach, if not continuously, then at some point in their sporting career. In Chapter

11: Coaching Relationships, we looked at how these coaching relationships can work most effectively.

The role of every coach, and all support staff, is to create a supportive environment in which champions feel confident and encouraged to give their best performances. For example, England football manager Sven Göran-Eriksson believes that his players need to feel confident to try new things, knowing they will not be criticized unfairly for daring to be brave on the pitch. Managers such as Eriksson will defend their players from the press and other critics and see that as part of their job.

However, this doesn't mean a coach shouldn't be tough if required. Coaches need to be able to tell their athletes if they aren't putting in the effort and commitment required. Coaches do need to inspire loyalty, trust and confidence to be effective. This means they need to adopt a coaching style that is true to themselves, and reflects their own personalities.

Most coaching relationships don't stay static, but develop naturally over time. When a sportsperson is younger they may need more guidance, but as they develop confidence and belief, they may start to challenge the coach. This can be a positive, productive relationship if both parties are willing to discuss their ideas openly. Renzie Hanham from mental conditioning specialists Gazing Performance says that some coaches are very directive all the time. Others are directive at the beginning of the relationship, but later on are keen for the athlete to take more and more responsibility. It depends on the processes of both the coach and the athlete.

Sometimes a champion will want to move onto a new coach in search of new insights. Sometimes the relationship will endure throughout the champion's career. There is no right or wrong approach.

Even though the coaching relationship can be an extremely close one, athletes will always need a sense of independence. In the end, they are the only person who can achieve the winning performance, and must have the self-belief and determination to do so.

Applications

- If you want a coach, whether for sporting purposes or as a life coach, make sure you find someone you respect and trust. You need to have confidence that the advice you are given is appropriate and well-founded.
- Don't be afraid to make your own suggestions or challenge your coach if you want to. A dynamic relationship can be extremely fulfilling for both parties.
- If you feel that your coach is no longer helping you, don't be afraid to end the relationship. You may have reached a point where you can do well on your own, or perhaps someone with a fresh perspective can be more useful.
- Try not to make your coach the scapegoat for your own shortcomings. In the end it's up to you to achieve your goals; no one else can do that for you.

Part IV
PEAK PERFORMANCE

Chapter 12

NERVE CONTROL

NERVES COME WITH THE TERRITORY of competing in top-level sport. Even the greatest champions can suffer from them. The question is, how do they cope with them effectively so that they can put in winning performances? The people who do that best are the people who become the world's champions.

CHAMPION NERVES

Former gold medal hurdler Sally Gunnell admits to having been so nervous that before a race she would sometimes end up in tears. She experienced so many emotions as a big competition drew closer but the worst day of all was perhaps the day before the heats. Once the heats got underway, Gunnell didn't feel so bad because the competition had finally started.

She would tell herself that there was no going back: 'This is your chance; if you don't do it now you're never going to get this opportunity again.' At the same time she would tell herself that whatever happened, people would still love her and be there for her.

When trying to relax Gunnell would lie on her bed, deep breathing and visualizing the coming race. She recalls the build-up to the 1992 Olympic final:

'I ran well in the semi-final. Then we had a rest day, which is awful, because you want to get on with it at that point and you're just waiting. It's the longest day in your life, just sitting around because you're scared of using up energy. I'd just try to sleep or go through the visualization. I was feeling quite confident, but at the same time quite nervy.

'Jon [Sally Gunnell's husband] never used to come out, except at the last minute, but he was always on the end of the phone. We would talk a lot. Bruce [Longden – coach] was also good. We would chat and he would always be very light-hearted. We wouldn't particularly chat about the race.

'As the race got nearer I got quieter and quieter. We'd do a little jog the day before. Then I'd try and sleep. But I couldn't sleep that night – your mind's very active, going through the race. I got up as late as possible, and had some food – force-fed myself. I was feeling so sick but I force-fed some bread and banana down my throat. Then I tried to give myself some quality thoughts again.

'I went back to my room. I had this routine of getting myself ready an hour beforehand – showering, doing my hair. Don't ask me why you do your hair and put make-up on, because you're only going to get all sweaty, but I suppose it's to do with wanting to feel good about yourself and building your confidence up. Once you start getting ready it's not so bad and you just stop yourself from letting any negative thoughts come at you. Then I'm meeting my coach and getting on the bus to go down to the track. I would go very

much inside myself and sit there totally nervous, but at the same time having to say to myself, "You can do this".

'Once you get to the track and start jogging around it's quite reassuring, because you've done the warm-up so many times. You have your routine of doing strides and stretching and so on.

'Of course, once you reach the track you start seeing all your competitors, and that's where the whole confidence game starts. That's where the arrogant side of me would come out. I would walk on tall and confident and I wouldn't sit in the corner. You can't let the others know you're as scared as they probably are. You're jumping around and saying "I can do this", not so much in words but in your whole attitude.

'I remember watching Sandra Farmer-Patrick hit a hurdle and thinking, "Eek, you could get hurt", and then doing a stride, telling myself it felt good. Bruce might then time me, but he'd lie like hell.

'All the time you're telling yourself you can do it. Negative thoughts would constantly come in, but you have to stop yourself thinking them. You tell yourself you've done everything right.

'The hardest part is when they call you and you have to go into the room to wait. All of a sudden you are on your own, without your coach. At that point you probably feel the loneliest person in the whole world.

'I used to think, "I don't want to do this. I'll go and hide." In Barcelona there was a little gate on the far side of the track. I remember thinking, "Why don't I just go out of that gate? No one's going to know. I could sneak out there and hide in the forest until it's all over." I was asking myself why I didn't have a normal nine-to-five job, and why I was putting myself under all this pressure. I wanted to be anywhere else but there at that moment, but I knew that the bottom line was I had to go through with it. All of a sudden you just want to get out there and just do it.'

As the organizers go through the required procedures of checking competitors' numbers and spikes, Gunnell concentrated on keeping calm.

'You see people who can't cope with the nervous situation, and that's what makes the difference between being a champion or not.

'Then you're marching out onto the track. You walk up to the start in front of 60,000 people. I kept my head down. I didn't dare look up and see the British flags, the people cheering me on. I didn't want to break my concentration. I was starting to get within myself.

'I walked up to the line and thought, "I've still got five minutes to go. What am I going to do with myself?" It was the longest five minutes ever in my whole life. I could hear people shouting my name: "Go on Sally, you can do it". I started to think about all the people at home.

'Then the whistle goes and you strip off down to your leotard, put your stuff in the box and are standing on the line. There's probably a minute to go and you can feel every heartbeat.'

That's when Sally's foundations of belief kicked in – and she had her sense of knowing that she would win.

'I'd been constantly saying to myself, "You can do this. You have done everything right. You've eaten well. You've done every training session possible. You've not been injured. You are 100%." Just before they said "On your marks" something inside me said, "This is it. This is your race. You can do this." And I really believed in those final seconds that I was going to win.'

THE VALUE OF NERVES

Sportspeople who do suffer from nerves shouldn't think they are unlucky. Former national athletics coach Frank Dick says there's nothing wrong with nerves. Athletes need the adrenalin that comes with them to make them sharp. Without that, he says, it's like trying to drive with low octane in your tank. There's nothing wrong with the sharpness that comes with being afraid. 'You need those bottom clenching moments!'

Round-the-world yachtswoman Ellen MacArthur always gets nervous before a race, but she doesn't see that as a bad thing. She says that the moment you stop feeling nervous is the moment you should stop racing. She believes that when you are racing across an ocean you have to have massive respect for your environment. Every time she sails out of a port she feel a sense of nervousness about whether everything will be OK, but she feels that keeps her on her toes.

MacArthur has no magic secret for mastering her nerves.

'The best thing is just to get out there and cross the start line. You concentrate on everything you have to do rather than worrying about saying goodbye to everyone and getting emotional about the fact you're not going to see everyone for two weeks or three months. You have to try and shut that out.'

Nerves shouldn't be seen as something to be avoided or driven totally away. Renzie Hanham from Gazing Principle says that nerves shouldn't be something that people feel they need to overcome. They are simply the body's natural response and trying to stop them is counterproductive. What matters is that the nervous feelings don't become overwhelming or divert the individual from their task. Former 400m champion Roger Black agrees. He believes you want the nerves to be there, but just need to make sure you don't let them overtake you.

Sprinter Mark Richardson sees nerves before a race as a natural and helpful thing. Though he suffers from nerves he believes that all athletes do and he doesn't see that as a problem. In fact, it's a great thing to have nerves, he says.

'You need those nerves to get the adrenalin and to get the most out of yourself. To keep a lid on it I use a technique called centring. I just concentrate on my breathing and do

*something that calms me down. I think music can affect
your moods, so if I feel that I'm almost too hyper pre-race,
I listen to some relaxing music – music that's just going to
bring me down a peg or two. And vice versa, if I don't feel
the competitive juices are flowing strongly enough before a
race, I'll listen to something that's going to pump me up a
bit. The choices tend to be between hip hop and R&B.'*

Richardson also draws on positive thinking when competing.
He remembers a positive time in the past and then tries to get
back into that state, thus generating the same positive outlook.
His aim is to achieve a relaxed state that allows for peak performance, one where he has a heightened sense of awareness
and arousal.

ACCEPTANCE OF NERVES

England rugby fly-half Jonny Wilkinson also admits to getting
incredibly nervous before any game he plays, whether international or club games. This is because, whether the team wins or
loses, he still has his own goals to complete. He has to satisfy
himself and his team-mates and fulfil his ambition inside that
particular game. A lot of his nerves come from knowing deep
down that he will be kicking in the match environment. He
knows it will be tough and there will be a lot of pressure. On
the other hand, he also sees this as being just his job. He says
that ever since he came into rugby he has thought of himself as
a kicker – that's his job.

When it comes to dealing with pre-match nerves, Wilkinson
just accepts they will be there.

*'I have tried recently to understand that I can't control these
nerves, and I shouldn't give in to them so badly. So before
an international game, when in the hotel, I will try to get
away from it for an hour. I might read a paper and try to find
a story to take my mind off it. I might watch some TV to stop
me thinking about things. When we are going to a game on
the coach, travelling for maybe an hour, I will look out of*

the window and think about people walking to the game. I keep my mind occupied, rather than thinking about the coming match, which I did for the first four or five years.'

Wilkinson is also making a conscious effort to remind himself that playing rugby is fun, not just a pressurized situation where he is constantly trying to do his best and meet his own high expectations.

'After a game I will sit in the changing room when the pressure is off and think, "Yeah, I enjoyed that and it feels fantastic". I feel proud and satisfied and that I can walk out with my shoulders back and my head up. Now I am trying to have that feeling more when I am out in the middle of a game, to think to myself that this is fun and it's what I want to do. I know that, but I don't necessarily realize it until it's all finished. It's a hard game and people take a lot of knocks, but when I am out there now I am trying to think that it's what I love doing; I'm only going to be doing it for a while, so I want to enjoy it.'

Golfing champion Nick Faldo isn't immune to nerves. He learnt how to deal with them during the course of his playing career.

'When you get nervous you tighten up. That's totally natural. It's your body's defences helping you – because you're in a nervous situation, it'll tighten up and won't move. As a golfer, you need to know that that's natural. You just need to turn a bit more, or your arms have got to keep moving, or that you've got to keep the tempo going. I learnt these things over time.'

Nerves are also part and parcel of racing for Olympic rower Matthew Pinsent, who describes himself as 'bubbling with nerves' in the last few minutes before a race starts. Pinsent describes what it feels like just before the starting gun.

'There are the two little voices in your head. One of them is telling you you're brave and the other one's telling you you're going to lose. I don't think that changes. I think it's quite universal. In some ways it's reassuring because it's the same again and again, almost irrespective of the quality of the race. At the Olympics it's extreme and it's stressful but one of the ways of dealing with it is to say, "Okay, this is good, this is what I need, this is part of the experience." You don't want to do it every day, but it's part of your body's preparation – the fact that you go through this horrendous state of nervous anxiety for hours and hours before the race. I've never necessarily been a big fan of trying to control the nerves; it's just part of it.'

As part of a rowing crew, Pinsent thinks it can be helpful to share your feelings with your team-mates.

'We have little conversations with each other about how we're feeling. It's definitely OK to say you're feeling nervous, or that you're not, or that you were good an hour ago but now you're struggling. It's nobody's fault if you're not nervous and it's nobody's fault if you are struggling with the nerves; it just helps to say it to someone else.'

Pinsent believes there is little you can do to relieve the nerves until you get into the warm-up stage in the last three quarters of an hour or so before the race. At that point you can finally start moving and going through a warm-up routine, but before that you've just got to sit there.

'You've just got to wait it out. You just try and concentrate on very simple things. The closer the race gets you try not to deal with everything at once. You certainly blank things out. People talk about controlling the controllables. You rule out stuff you can't control, whether that's the weather or to a certain extent the opposition, the crowd, or the status of the event. If you're nervous those things become very important. But you have to say, "Okay, it's just a rowing race. We

can win this and the way we're going to win this is by doing these two or three things very well."'

Once a race is underway, holding your nerve is just as important as it is before the start. Matthew Pinsent knows that if another boat gets a lead early on, it's vital not to panic and overreact.

'You need to have rehearsed enough or be experienced enough to know that panicking doesn't work. You're probably telling yourself that they've worked harder than you to get out into the lead and that they are just as tired as you are. It's a matter of making them pay for that effort. You also need good leadership and communication within the crew to make sure that panic doesn't set in and that you don't chase the race. You have to row your own race to a certain extent. It's no good beating off that boat's challenge and doing something different to get back level with them, and then finding that they weren't judging the race right anyway.

'Of course it depends where in the race it's happening and which crew it is. In a six-boat final there are going to be two crews who are thinking that they are fifth and sixth quickest and out of the medals; their only tactic is just to go for it and get out in front. Every now and then they may make the favourites panic, in which case the tactic has worked. So you have to be aware that may be going on in the race.'

Adrian Moorhouse says that he certainly felt a heightened adrenalin surge during the build-up to the Olympic final in Seoul in 1988. However, he tried to manage his nervous energy so that it was there for the race, rather than wasting it beforehand. This ability to manage the energy takes advanced practice, so that the mental inner chatter can be steered in a positive direction. Negative thoughts may come in, but they only last a split second.

Moorhouse recalls the last half hour before the race, where he simply tried to put the final in perspective.

'I was in a room with seven guys, just looking at them and thinking human things: "It's not the end of the world; this is just seven guys; they've all got families; they all want to have a bit of a race." I reminded myself of the big things in the world that were going on. I reminded myself of people I'd lost who were close to me, or who were ill, and thinking, "Why am I getting worried?"'

PHYSICAL RELEASE

Former Davis Cup tennis captain David Lloyd accepts that everybody gets nervous before an important sporting competition. In his career he developed a physical way of dealing with his pre-match nervous energy.

'I never controlled my nerves. I would go out on the practice court and play full out for half an hour. That meant I went on the match court slightly tired and warm as hell. Just by being slightly tired I found it took a bit of the edge off. So I played a set or a set and a half before going on court and that helped me.'

Michael Lynagh, former Australian rugby captain, also used physical activity as a way of coping with his nerves before a game.

'I always tried to do something physical on the morning of a match, maybe just going for a walk. Before a game in Scotland once I played ping-pong for a good hour. That was great fun and just released some nervous energy.

'One of the things Dad taught me at an early age was that when people get nervous they get very closed – they don't talk and don't want to mix. So I used to go after break-fast and make a point of sitting in the public areas of the

hotel – not right by the door, but in public and I would read papers. People would come and say hello.'

When driving to a match on the bus Lynagh was usually fairly relaxed, but if he began feeling particularly nervous he would close his eyes and run through his mental rehearsal routine – which would sometimes put him to sleep. Then, when the team reached the ground, Lynagh would definitely start getting nervous, but he accepted the feeling was there was a reason. He would always acknowledge how he was feeling. He often made a point telling the younger guys that he was feeling a bit nervous that day and asking the how they felt. Sharing feelings in this was helpful, he found, and much better than trying to bury the nerves.

In the next chapter we look at how champions can use routines to help them manage their nervous energy, before and during competition.

Chapter 13

THE ROCK OF ROUTINE

WHEN TRYING TO PUT IN A PEAK PERFORMANCE, sporting champions make effective use of routines. These can be used to help them cope with highly pressured moments, as noted in Chapter 9, or to generally keep nerves at a positive level. They also provide a familiar build-up to the start of a match or a contest. They provide a rock of support in moments of pressure.

PRE-MATCH ROUTINES

Sports psychologist John Syer works with athletes to assist them in identifying routines that support their build-up to performing and help them to create the right mental state. He questions athletes to help them become more aware of what they do in their routine. In this way the athlete may identify something important that they weren't aware of. It may be something they want to continue doing or to change.

Syer doesn't think there is one right way to prepare, whether a week before, three days before, the day before or on the day. There is no routine that works for everybody, though there probably is for the individual, he says.

> *'My prime concern is to help my clients to become aware of what they are currently doing because, until they know what they are doing, they can't change anyway. If you help me to become aware of what I'm doing, I might be appalled but I'm also deeply interested because suddenly I have all sorts of new options.'*

Sports psychologist Professor Graham Jones has also worked with sporting top performers to help them with their build-up routines. He has helped them to recognize what works and what doesn't work, by asking them to think about past good performances and identifying common things that they did. The sportspeople can also think about past performances that were not so good and again identify any common actions or factors in the build-up. Professor Jones says that the athletes can come up with absolutely anything – what they had for breakfast or what time they went to bed the night before. Once the athlete has identified the things they associate with successful performances, they can try to recreate or do those things next time they compete. If they do so, they should feel better about the competition and their potential to do well.

Some routines are akin to superstitions. For example, tennis genius Bjorn Borg never shaved during the Wimbledon championship. Professor Jones says:

> *'At some stage he associated not shaving with performing well. It's important for most performers to have things that they associate with success, and that they try to replicate every time they compete. You try to get people into routines, and they might begin days before they perform well. As you get closer you can use triggers or breathing techniques,*

centring techniques and so on. It has to be specific to the
individual's needs.'

The important thing is to identify the factors that really make
a difference in terms of supporting a performance and not to
get distracted by irrelevancies. Sometimes people can read
too much into a certain routine, and the influence it has over
the final result. England football coach Sven-Göran Eriksson
says:

> *'When I was a player in the second division, for one period*
> *we played better football away than we did at home. So the*
> *manager called us in two hours earlier than normal before*
> *our next home game, put us on a bus and took us for an*
> *hour's ride. It didn't work.'*

That unnecessary trip was abandoned before the next home
match.

In his football playing days, former England Under-21 coach
David Platt found it difficult waiting for a match to start.

> *'People prepare in different ways before a game. I was qui-*
> *eter. The hour before the game dragged on for me. I'd go*
> *in the dressing room 75 minutes before the game and it*
> *dragged on. I was relaxed. I wasn't boisterous or bouncing*
> *around. By the time I'd read the programme and had a*
> *massage I had half an hour to kill. I'd think, "What am I*
> *going to do now?" I just wanted to play.'*

Platt doesn't like the teams he coaches now to be disturbed
before a match.

> *'I don't like people coming into my dressing room who aren't*
> *involved in that particular game. I have thrown photogra-*
> *phers out. You can disturb people. I think players are very*
> *focused in that hour between two o'clock and three o'clock.*
> *They are focused within routines. Some people will laugh*
> *and joke, but that is their routine. At Nottingham Forest*

*we had a couple of players who put earphones on and just
sat there. People have different ways of getting themselves
ready for a game.'*

While some people will use a routine to keep themselves sufficiently calm, others may need to increase their excitement
levels. Sports psychologist John Syer says:

*'When I was at Tottenham in the early 1980s, Ray Clemence
was goalkeeper. He was probably the oldest and most experienced player in the team. On the day of a league match,
he would to start warming up way before anybody else.
(The peak of this warm-up was dancing from foot to foot,
dressed only in his underpants, repeating the mantra "One
for all and all for one" over and over again!) He needed
this routine and a long build-up to reach an optimal level
of excitement. On the other hand, when he was injured,
Tony Parkes chose to find a quiet place in the shower room
where he could calm down until some 20 minutes before
the game. This was his way of reaching an optimum level
of excitement.'*

England rugby captain Lawrence Dallaglio developed his pre-
match routine over time, as he discovered what worked for
him.

*'You pick things up and leave other things behind and you
develop a framework over a period of time. All sportsmen
have rituals. And when you become successful there are
certain preparations you tend to stick to, which become
your own personal blueprint for success. The older you get
and the more experienced you become, you add and sub-
tract from the blueprint. Within a team sport that blueprint
has to be flexible to incorporate other people's blueprints as
well; what works for me might not necessarily work for the
guy I am playing with. You have to respect that.'*

NEED FOR FLEXIBILITY

Even when a sportsperson has developed a routine that suits them, they have to be able to adapt it to circumstances on the day. For example, after breakfast on match day England rugby captain Lawrence Dallaglio likes to relax and do his own thing, given the limitations imposed by the timetable for the team, such as the time for setting off for the ground.

'You can't always control things, but you have your own framework that you mix with what is required for the team. And you have to have a preparation routine that can adapt to kick-off being delayed, for example. Anything can happen to throw you out of your normal routine. It happens more often when you play away from home because you are less in control.'

Breaststroke champion Adrian Moorhouse found himself using up lots of emotional energy before the Olympic final in Seoul in 1988. Unusually, the final was the day after the heats, rather than on the same day – a change in routine he didn't like.

'I'd never before gone to sleep between the heat and the final and that challenged me. I couldn't stop my visualization tape, which was a problem. The next morning I got up at five and went through my race day routine. I remember wanting it to be over because it was mine to win. I felt that I wanted to get it out of my system. I couldn't wait to do it and was using up too much emotional energy straining at the leash.

'So I did a lot of relaxation, minimizing what it meant – the Olympic factor. I just focused on the process. I thought about how I would step on the block, what I would do if there was a false start, how I would dive. I just concentrated on all the processes and got away from the Olympic aspect.'

Olympic multiple gold medal-winning rower Matthew Pinsent understands that it can prove a weakness to be too dependent on a routine. Pinsent says of his crew:

> *'We definitely have a routine in terms of how we warm up and when we warm up, but beyond that I try not to have too fixed an idea of what's going to happen, just because I want to be as flexible and adaptable as possible. I'm certainly not superstitious. If anything, I'm superstitious about not being superstitious. You do all this training and then suddenly get upset at the last minute because you put your socks on the wrong way round ...*
>
> *'Sometimes you're not given the same build-up to each race. Maybe something unforeseen happens, or the weather may change and the timing for the transport changes, so your routine might be knocked slightly. You have to sort out exactly what the ingredients of success are and I don't think it's about having a certain breathing routine 90 minutes beforehand and so on. You can't rely on those things. Gold medals are won in large amount in the training you do, not in the last minute. Okay, the last minute things are important, but only in their generality. Eventually you've got to arrive on the start line ready to race and pretty much warmed up. How you do that is up to you. I could change my routine, change my ideas, but that wouldn't make any difference. I'd hope I'd still win.'*

Routines can also be limiting if they clash with someone else's. Sports psychologist John Syer recalls just such a problem. Some years ago he worked with a football player who had a routine that required him to be the last player out of the dressing room. Towards the end of his career he changed clubs and unfortunately someone there had the same routine. Clearly it wasn't possible for both players to be last out. The result? A problem.

Syer suggests that, in such situations, athletes need only to identify the feeling their routine evokes. Once they can name that feeling they can think of alternative methods of evoking it. If the football player realizes that leaving the dressing room last makes him feel calm or in control or strong, he may consider what sort of conversation, music, object, sentence or physical movement gives him the same feeling and build attention to this into his old routine. This is the kind of 'anchor' and 'trigger' approach considered in Chapter 8.

FAMILIARITY

Routines are valuable partly because they are familiar to the individual concerned. They increase the sense of security they feel in a potentially stressful time. Similarly, having a sense of familiarity about your surroundings, however you achieve it, can be a major help.

The value of familiarity is that it increases the sportsperson's sense of comfort. Most footballers would rather play at home, for example, because it's their patch. The advantage that familiarity with the home ground gives a team is undeniable. David Platt Platt, former England football captain and Under-21 England coach, says:

'You can't beat playing at home. Home advantage is the familiarity. The pitch might be exactly the same size at Villa Park as it is at Manchester United, but the advertising boards are different, the stands are different. At home the advertising boards give you an awareness of where you are on the pitch.'

Sports psychologist Professor Graham Jones agrees that familiarity is what home advantage is about. If you're playing in a familiar environment, you know the level at which you can control the environment, Professor Jones says. You don't have to worry about certain aspects of it. In contrast, when you are playing away from home, you don't know what to expect. That is why coaches talk about 'silencing the crowd' early on, because they know they need to get some control over the environment. Professor Jones recalls the Six Nations match between Wales and Italy in 2001.

> *'On paper Wales should beat Italy every time, but the Italians haven't been part of the Six Nations for very long and they always raise their game. So we talked about killing the Italians off early on so they couldn't come back. In the first 20 minutes Wales took a significant lead, which the Italians couldn't claw back. It's about suppressing the crowd and controlling the environment. Knowing you've got control over things is so important.'*

Professor Jones stresses the importance of creating a conducive environment – one that allows people to focus on what they need to do, which is to perform, and not to have to worry about anything else. What matters is controlling the controllables, controlling the environment to enable people to perform at their maximum level.

Some sportspeople will make an extra effort to familiarize themselves with the environment in which they will be competing.

Michael Lynagh, former Australian rugby captain, made a special effort to go and practise kicking in the ground where he was shortly due to play. When playing professionally he developed a regular routine for kicking practice before a match.

> *'I found it really helped me to go down the afternoon before and kick in the conditions at the ground at the same time that we would be playing. It just made sense. I'd have three kicks from in front of the goal posts about 20 yards out, then three kicks from the junction of the 22 and the 15 yard lines on both sides. Then I'd have three more about 40 yards out. Then I would turn around and do the same thing at the other end. If you are familiar with the territory, it just makes you feel a little bit more comfortable.'*

In the next chapter we consider another way that sporting champions rely on themselves – by keeping their inner voice positive.

Chapter 14

POSITIVE TALK

WHEN IT COMES TO DELIVERING A PEAK PERFORMANCE, sporting champions have to remain positive about themselves and their ability to win. Their inner voice needs to be feeding them positive thoughts about what they are about to do.

POSITIVE SPIN

Champions have the ability to keep their inner voice positive. They see their environment and what happens to them in a positive light. They interpret the world in a way that supports them and encourages them to strive for success.

Performance expert and sports psychologist Professor Graham Jones has noted the ability of elite performers to put a positive spin on situations. He says that self-esteem is a big factor in helping them maintain that positive outlook, but it can be easily knocked. However, the world's best have complete control of how they feel about themselves and they don't take things personally. They take negative feedback as a way to improve. In effect they can control how they think. Professor Jones says:

> *'I used to work with an England batsman who was well known for scratching around a bit early in his innings. The opposition knew they had to get him out early because once he was set, they were in trouble. But he would play and miss a lot early on in the innings. This batsman would attribute it to the pitches and so on, when in fact he was playing abysmally. But he was maintaining his self-belief. He would think: "It's not anything to do with me. This ball is swinging around and moving all over the place."*
>
> *'When he was eventually out he would reappraise and think there was perhaps something going on that wasn't right and he should get in the nets and sort it out. Elite people have that kind of control over what they're thinking. It's called self-serving bias. It's when you're saying, "It's nothing to do with me. There's nothing wrong with me." But once you get off the ground you get straight in the nets and work on what was going wrong.'*

Putting a positive spin on a situation is a way of 'reframing' it to find the silver lining in the cloud. Renzie Hanham from Gazing Performance Limited recalls an experience with a Seido karate world champion where he was able to turn a bad situation into a positive one.

> *'This guy was in line to win the middleweight championship, but then he tore his hamstring. That's a devastating thing to happen because it means you can't use your legs. But I told him about a judo champion who won his title with a broken leg. It was a lie.*
>
> *'Then I reframed the situation by telling the injured karate competitor that he was actually making mistakes*

when he was kicking and so he should be using his hands.
He went on to win the championship.'

NLP trainer Graham Shaw also believes that negative thoughts can be converted into positive ones. He recalls a Danish professional triathlete called Morten Fenger who was explaining what it was like to complete a triathlon – and how much it hurt. But Fenger was able to see this pain positively, Shaw says. Fenger would tell himself that if he could feel that he was hurting so much, that meant he was alive – and wasn't it wonderful to be alive! In this way Fenger was able to use the pain he was feeling to get himself into a positive state again.

Of course, there are times when a little negative voice can prove productive. Shaw recalls his own experience of running the 10km road race in the World Masters Championships in Italy when he was 49 years old. When he arrived at the start of the race he felt positive because he had spent so much time visualizing and preparing for this moment. Then during the race he used a little bit of a negative prompt. Shaw knew from experience that the toughest part of the race for him was the stretch between 5km and 8km. That's when he began to hurt and started to wilt.

'I used some self-talk, which was this: "You haven't spent £400 and flown all this way to be sitting in the bar afterwards with the athletes, having got a bad time, regretting for the other four days you are out here that you didn't make it hurt and put the effort in here." I made a picture. I said to myself: "You've got all the rest of the week to sit and put your feet up, so get in there now and damn well just do it."

'A lot of people get motivated by the "away from" impulse – a negative image – and that's how I boosted myself during that race. Sometimes people need negative images to give themselves a thump. For me it was a massive "away from" that made me put up with the pain. I could go through the pain because I couldn't face the thought of sitting there talking to other people about having achieved a terrible time.'

The negative prompt worked well. Shaw beat his 'acceptable' target time by 15 seconds.

CONFIDENCE TECHNIQUES

Simply standing in a confident manner and presenting yourself positively has an impact on how you feel. As NLP trainer Graham Shaw says, there are techniques that can be used for keeping the inner voice positive. One very simple technique uses the relationship between physiology and mental state. For example, if you sit with your shoulders slumped and head down, you are more likely to feel fed up or miserable. If you sit up, with your shoulders back a little, you tend to feel more positive. If you get people to stand in a more confident manner, they start to feel more confident.

Modern pentathlete Dr Stephanie Cook used to act confidently, even when she was feeling under pressure. She particularly worked on improving her confidence in fencing, which she found to be one of the more difficult events.

> *'If I lost a few hits in a row, my self-confidence would diminish and that would result in me fencing more defensively and consequently not so well. I worked on a way of dealing with defeat, so that I still walked on with my head up, looking as confident as ever to my opponents. By continuing to act confidently, this kept my determination and confidence strong.'*

In addition to physical or physiological techniques, another method for cutting down negative internal dialogue – or any internal dialogue – is to divert attention to the outside world. NLP trainer Graham Shaw says:

> *'You could get a conference presenter to look at a dot on the wall, standing upright and feeling good. While they look at the dot, get them to notice that they can see the corners of the room – that's their peripheral vision. They can bring their vision down to notice everybody in the room. As a con-*

ference presenter, their attention is now out on the group. They have a heightened awareness of what's happening out there, which they need as a presenter to give themselves feedback. What they don't want is voices in their head saying, "How am I going to do this?" So in this way they have cut down their internal dialogue.'

Sometimes a champion might want to keep their attention focused within, rather than on the external world. Former sprinter John Regis says that any small negative thought could become 'the size of an avalanche' once you were in the arena before a race. Regis would try to avoid negative thoughts occurring and keep his thinking positive before a race by not letting himself worry about what other people were doing, or how fast they seemed to be running when warming up.

'I used to look at people running, but when you look at people running, everyone looks really quick. So I stopped doing that. I would sit looking at the floor, so I couldn't see what people were doing and I kept all my energies within me. They couldn't affect me and I could focus more on what I needed to do.'

Former badminton champion Gill Clark used to keep up her positive attitude by developing an attacking game strategy.

'You study the opponent, and you know tactically what they're good at.

'Every coach would tell you not to serve to your opponent's strengths. But, because I'm a bit of a funny one, I think, "Right, she's left-handed and she always likes to play this brush return; she's going to play it now on my backhand side. So, the first serve I'm going to do, I'm going to play to her strength."

'That way your opponent is going to think, "Heck, she's returned my best shot, I'd better not play my best shot any more." So I've got the mental edge right at the start of the

match, because now she is afraid to play her best shot. So
we can take her best shot out of the game.'

STAY IN THE NOW

When golfing champion Nick Faldo won the British Open at
Muirfield in 1992 he started out feeling extremely positive, but
then things began to slip. Somehow he managed not to dwell
on what had gone before but kept concentrating on what he
needed to do now to take the championship. At the time he
was world number two, had just won a tournament in Ireland
and he was feeling confident. Faldo recalls the event vividly:

'I'm playing great and I'm hot favourite to win. I thought,
"Yes, this is my week to win again". I opened with 66, 64 and
had a four shot lead. Then on the Sunday all of a sudden
I got reeled in. I started making some mistakes. I bogeyed
the eleventh. I three putted the thirteenth. After that I said
to Fanny [Sunesson – caddy], "You know, I'm alright. You
know I'm alright." Then on the fourteenth I hit straight into
the bunker. I kept saying, "I don't know what's going on but
I'm alright." Then I looked at the leaderboard and I was
two back.

'But one of the tricks I was working on that week was
to forget everything. I suddenly said to myself, "OK, forget
everything that's happened over the whole week, good or
bad. Just forget it. It's all gone. You've got four holes to play;
you better play the best four holes of your life."

'I'm now walking off the fourteenth green to tee off on
the fifteenth. I hit the famous five iron, a little half shot
which finished three foot from the hole. On the seventeenth
I hit an absolutely perfect drive with a four iron. The best
you could do was to get 20 foot left of the hole and I hit it
right there and two putted for a birdie.

'Now I'm tired and then I heard an almighty groan from
the eighteenth and I just sensed that John Cook had taken
five. You've got a hundred yard walk to the eighteenth. Every
step I said "You've got four to win, four to win." And then I

hit two perfect shots. The second, with a three iron, I hit one of my greatest, best shots, straight at the pin. Then I made a two putt and I won.'

Former England footballer Alan Shearer had a great ability not to dwell on missed shots. He would remain positive and concentrate on the present moment of the game, a skill that impresses former England captain David Platt. Platt says:

'When Alan misses a chance he just "blows" it away. He breathes and it is gone. He sniffs up his nose and that is his way of saying it's gone. He just moves on from there thinking he'll get another chance, he'll get another goal. That's the mental strength of the man and that's why he is one of the leading goal scorers every year.'

PSYCHING OUT

Part of the process of staying positive involves not getting distracted by any psyching out games that the opposition try to use.

Sally Gunnell recalls waiting in the call room after warming up before the 1992 Olympic 400m hurdles final. She kept her cool and exuded confidence, regardless of what was happening around her. Gunnell says:

'All the finalists are in there psyching each other out. I remember Sandra Farmer-Patrick strutting her stuff, moaning about this and that and giving me daggers. I was thinking, "Right, I'm in charge here." I would give off an aura. I don't know how I did it, but I was just lying there with my legs up on the wall, saying I was conserving energy. Everyone else would be charging around. But I was thinking: "I've warmed up, I've done everything I can do. There's nothing else that could get me prepared. I am in total control." This is the message I was giving out to everybody.'

When it comes to psyching out others, the greatest champions don't tend to do it as a result of some strategy; they just behave with instinctive confidence that can have a negative impact on other competitors with perhaps lesser self-belief.

Former national athletics coach Frank Dick thinks what matters is simply to be totally competitive – something the athlete has practised through visualization or mental rehearsal beforehand.

> '*We practise being totally competitive because when you go out to compete, it's not just a physical thing; it's everything about you. Daley Thompson would chat to people and I'm not sure he ever thought of it as consciously psyching somebody out. If you start getting involved in the notion that that's what you have got to do, you know you're a loser. You're dealing with the tricks of the trade before you've delivered the trade. You do these things instinctively – it's part of the competition, part of the drive.*'

Athletics coach Ron Roddan, who worked with 100m champion Linford Christie, knows that a lot of psyching out goes on in the final run-up to a race. About 20 minutes before a race the athletes leave their coaches in the warm-up area and go into the control room. Roddan says:

> '*In that room a lot of things happen. A lot of mind games go on. Linford told me that some people came out shaking. Some people have such a strong aura that it puts other people off. Another coach told his athletes to stay away from Linford in the control room because he had that effect just by being there.*'

Christie clearly had a natural ability to put weaker opponents off by his sense of self-belief. Sometimes, however, he would proactively try to make a point to his rivals. After Christie won 100m gold in the Barcelona Olympics in 1992 some American athletes started saying he wouldn't have won if Carl Lewis, the world record holder, had been competing. Christie was not amused.

By the time of the World Championships at Stuttgart the following year, 1993, Andre Cason was number one and Lewis still held the world record. Christie was up against them both and determined to prove a point. Roddan recalls Christie's attitude to those World Championships.

> 'Linford said, "Let's go to the warm-up". Cason was there doing starts and long runs. Carl Lewis was there. Linford took his top off and started warming up in Cason's lane. He made Cason run round him. Straight away, Cason had lost the race. I had never seen Linford do that before. He then walked back to me and said, "It's time. Let's go." He didn't like the Americans because of their attitudes; they said he wouldn't have won the Olympics and he wanted to prove a point. And he did it in the best way possible.'

Christie won the 100m final in 9.87 seconds, pushing Cason into second place (a time of 9.92 seconds). Lewis was fourth in a time of 10.02 seconds. Christie was, understandably, delighted.

When champions such as Christie deliver such top performances they sometimes describe themselves as having been 'in the zone'. In the next chapter we look at what elite sportspeople mean by this, and whether they can enter the state at will.

Chapter 15

INTO THE ZONE

CHAMPION ATHLETES OFTEN REFER to the almost mythical desired state of being 'in the zone'. But what exactly do they mean by that?

THE ZONE EXPLAINED

Former sprinter Mark Richardson talks about being in the zone when in the winter of 1996, after suffering from food poisoning, he forced his way into the 4×400m relay team. Running the last leg in 43.60 seconds, he recorded the fastest relay split in the final of all the competitors and the fastest relay split ever run by a British athlete. So what is it like to be 'in the zone'? Richardson describes it thus:

'It's a very strange feeling. It's as if time slows down and you see everything so clearly. You just know that everything about your technique is spot on. It just feels so effortless; it's almost as if you're floating across the track. Every muscle, every fibre, every sinew is working in complete harmony and the end product is that you run fantastically well.'

Champion hurdler Sally Gunnell says she only entered the zone twice – once when winning Olympic gold in Barcelona in 1992, and then when winning the world championships a year later.

'What I call being in the zone is when the gun goes and I don't remember any of the race. It's dreamlike. My mind just switches off. You go into automatic pilot. I don't remember what happened down the back straight; I don't remember going over the eighth hurdle or even crossing the line.'

Sports psychologist Steve Sylvester says that such a lack of memory is quite common amongst sportspeople who manage to get into the zone. Sometimes they can't remember what they actually did, because they've tuned in to it and done it without thought. This is a characteristic of being totally connected to your performance – so much so that you can't remember the detail of it, because you're flowing, you're not processing, Sylvester says. If you're not processing on a conscious level, it's harder to remember what you actually did.

Former sprinter John Regis describes what being in the zone felt like to him:

'It was the belief and knowledge that you were going to run a very good race. It didn't always necessarily mean you were going to win, but it meant that the consistency of the performance was going to be at the highest level.'

When in the zone, time seemed to go into slow motion. Regis says:

'It felt as though I was running the replay, when it's slowed down. It didn't feel like 19 seconds. It's like you are going through a time warp, going back in time and seeing everything that's going on. It feels like slow motion. It's a strange feeling.

'A gun could be fired next to me and I wouldn't hear it – you're so in tune with what you need to be doing. I can feel everybody's strength, everybody's power, if they are able to turn it on or not. At the same time I'm doing what I have to do. When you get that feeling, you are totally in control.'

GETTING INTO THE ZONE

The big question, of course, is how do you get into the zone? Former sprinter Mark Richardson's experience was that mainly it 'just happens'. He says you can use visualization to try and help you get in the zone in the race, but in reality it's just something you fall into. Richardson says when it clicks in, it's the most natural place in the world to be.

Similarly, champion hurdler Sally Gunnell never had a method for deliberately getting into the zone. She says:

'I don't think it's something you can put yourself into; it just happens. There are lots of feelings that go with it: confidence and belief, things like that. It just happened twice for me – in the 1992 Olympics and the 1993 World Championships. The other years when I won titles, such as the Europeans in 1994, I wasn't in the zone. In the Europeans I can remember bits and pieces of the race, being in the back straight, coming off the eighth hurdle. I wasn't in the zone.'

Sports psychologist and performance expert Professor Graham Jones acknowledges that there is no straightforward way to get yourself into the zone at will. If it was easy, every sportsperson would be in the zone all the time. His recommendation is to recognize what you associate with good performances and what you associate with bad performances and then get rid of all the bad performance associations; you work with everything you've done that's associated with good performances. You need to replicate those factors to give yourself the best chance to let a good performance happen. Professor Jones says:

> *'You want people to be relaxed mentally and to feel in control and you don't want them to worry about the process. You want them to know what the process is, and just do it.*
>
> *'People will know very early on whether they're in the zone or not, but there's no answer to how you get someone there. You just know what makes you perform well and you give yourself the best possible opportunity – then you just hope.'*

THE SUPERSTATE

Javelin champion Steve Backley has been in the zone on several occasions. One such time was during the 2002 European Championships in Munich, where he took the gold medal. Backley says of his win:

> *'It was a very conscious, controlled performance. That's what being in the zone means for me. It's accessing something above and beyond normal successful behaviour.'*

Backley believes that in competition, success goes to the individual most able to manage his or her mood or state. As he says, when you've got 12 or 15 healthy guys, all capable of delivering a high level of performance, you have to access the states that optimize performance to win the gold medal. That's the skill.

Backley believes that this ability to access the required state is what makes the difference between great athletes and the real champions – whom he calls 'warriors'.

For Backley, the perfect state is what he calls a 'superstate'. He recalls his first experience of entering a 'superstate'. The year was 1990 and he had just won his first European gold medal. Immediately afterwards he went to compete in Budapest and though tired, he realized he dearly wanted to win the competition. He promised himself he would do his best and then rest afterwards.

> 'I'd had a bit of an unbeaten streak at this time. I came into the first round and threw about 82m, which ordinarily would have been enough to win. Then this big Russian guy stepped up and did 82.90 to go ahead. I'd already taken my boots off and I totally lost focus. I was out of the zone.
>
> 'When the Russian went ahead of me I just saw red, metaphorically speaking. I put my boots back on and as I was doing that there seemed to be a subliminal tape in my conscious mind that was dealing with all the peripheral stuff. It was like I was just watching what was going on. From that moment for the next minute and a half I was in this superstate. I put my boots back on, walked out to the javelin and went through the normal procedure, but it was all as if I was two or three feet behind and looking down on myself. I don't remember running in.
>
> 'The result was 85.90m – a British record.
>
> 'I came away a bit spooked, but it made me ask questions. What happened there?'

Backley believes the superstate is the result of extreme anxiety or pressure to achieve – the result of a flight or fight situation, coupled with the belief that you can come out on top. It isn't just athletes who experience it, Backley believes, but ordinary people in a traumatic situation, perhaps caught up in some major disaster.

Having experienced the superstate in Budapest, Backley wanted to be able to achieve it again.

> 'I was thinking that if I can get there again by choice, I can do whatever I want. That for me is the Holy Grail. I have a better understanding of it now and an ability to access it. I have used it since but it isn't easy. You need a certain set of circumstances. You need to be healthy and to have great, stable preparation. I can't turn it on immediately, from one

second to the next. In a major championship I will gather
this state over about three or four weeks.'

Backley also believes that the superstate is accessed out of
adversity, not out of success or pleasure. An athlete who has
just put in a poor performance and so increased pressure on
himself is more likely to access it than one on a roll of top
performances.

The process that Backley has developed to try and access
the superstate during competition centres around self-analysis. He asks himself questions about his performance and
technique and answers them in ways that reinforce the desired
result. For example, when throwing the javelin Backley needs
to keep his left shoulder in a certain position, across his body.
So he asks himself, 'Why am I doing this?' The real reason in
terms of technique is to stop himself spinning out of line, but
he might give himself another reason, that he is slightly embar-
rassed coming in to the throw. He says: 'I answer myself with
a very rational answer that will reinforce why I am putting my
left side away.'

It is essential, however, to avoid derogatory questions that
can reinforce a negative reaction. Asking, 'Why didn't I train
right?' is not helpful. Asking 'What do I need for 85 on my next
throw?' is more positive. Backley says: 'Then you're off to a
positive start because you are looking at a positive outcome.'
For Backley, as a competition approaches, the result of continued questioning can be to push his mind into overdrive. He can
also start feeling tired. This isn't bad news, though. He knows
then that the superstate is about to come out. He says:

'It's almost a bit of Star Wars *stuff – it's the force. It's*
because you are becoming a warrior and it's an amazing
thing.'

When competing in the 2000 Olympics, Backley could sense
the superstate coming on.

*'I had a growing sense that I was going to do something.
What really set me off was when I got my key and went to
my room. There was my bag on the bed. I was on the top
floor and I went to the window and opened the curtains. I
looked straight through the window of the house opposite,
which was directly lined up with the house opposite it, and
it framed the Olympic flag on the staging. It was about half
a mile away. Talk about the hairs standing up on the back
of your neck. There was the Olympic flag right smack bang
at my bedroom window. I thought a superstate was coming
on.'*

In the Olympics Backley performed well, beating the previous
Olympic record, before being pushed into silver.

Backley accessed his winning state again in the European
Championships in Munich in August 2002, where he took gold
– for the fourth time in a row. The achievement came hard
on the heels of a gold medal in the Commonwealth Games
in Manchester in July. Backley says that his preparation for
Munich began before the Commonwealth competition had
actually finished. In fact, it started as soon as the first round was
completed. Having thrown 86.81m, Backley was way ahead of
the rest of the field and knew that he had won.

*'In the next round I was thinking, "You've got Munich next
week. You've got a qualification requirement of 83m. What
is the best way for you to qualify?" It was like I was asking
myself a series of questions.'*

Backley began forming a plan for how he would achieve the
required qualification throw. He then used the second round
in the Manchester Commonwealth Games to practise his
qualification throw for Munich. Then he stopped throwing
altogether.

*'I had already won, and I'd practised my qualification
throw. I asked myself, "Is there anything more to be gained*

from this competition? No. Is there anything to lose? Yes,
you could get hurt. So stop."'

Backley says he 'turned his back' on the rest of the competition
in Manchester and has hardly any memories of it. His preparations for the European Championships then continued.

'I practised the qualifying throw and had a conversation
going on in my mind. The fact that I'd won the last three
was in the back of my mind, but I didn't focus on it like
that. It was more in terms of "This is mine, you can't have
it. This is meant to be. This is my baby. I haven't lost one of
these." I was developing a kind of love affair with the event.
"If you're going to try and take this off me, you will lose.
There's no way I'm going to let you take this easily." It's a
feeling of really going to war.'

When the European Championships in Munich got underway,
Backley achieved the required qualification distance and then
began gearing up for the final, gradually developing his superstate.

Believing that sleep is vital for storing up energy and supporting the superstate, Backley slept during the day of the
final. He admits he may have slept too much, because he felt
a bit groggy during his warm up and wasn't throwing as well
as he would like. He still felt somewhat sleepy during the
first round, but put in a reasonable throw of 88.29m and took
second place.

'I knew there was more to come. The first throw was good,
but it wasn't as fast as I could have done. It was quite a con-
trolled throw – I didn't lash through it. The second throw
was my worst on the day and slightly tailed. That made me
focus on alignment and being faster on the runway, so I had
a plan. If you have a plan, belief and want it enough, it's
going to happen.'

The third throw went further, but it was in the fifth round that Backley brought everything together, throwing a mighty 88.54m to take the lead and win gold.

Even when top sportspeople don't feel they have entered that wonderful state of being 'in the zone', they still need to remain highly focused during competitions. We examine how champions create and maintain such focus in the next chapter.

Chapter 16

FOCUS AND REFOCUS

IT IS GENERALLY ACCEPTED that sport's greatest champions have a supreme ability to maintain their focus during competition.

But what is 'focus'? What does it mean when sportspeople say they need to maintain their focus? Former national athletics coach Frank Dick relates this anecdote by way of explanation:

> *'When Babe Ruth was in his last season in baseball he was in a batting slump. He wasn't playing well and the team was in danger of going out of the World Series. Ruth was two strikes down and he was given a bit of verbal by some guy behind him. Ruth replied by telling the guy to watch the green out there, because that was where the ball was going.*

Well, with a bit of licence, that's where the ball went. Ruth got a home run.

'Ruth was asked later about what he was thinking when he was standing on the plate. Was he thinking, this is my last chance, with two strikes down? Was he thinking about the guy giving him a hard time? Was he thinking that if this went wrong, he'd be out?

'Ruth said he wasn't thinking of any of these things – "I was thinking about hitting the ball".

'That's what focus is.'

VITAL FOCUS

Javelin champion Steve Backley appreciates the importance of generating and maintaining his focus before a competition begins. He likens the period after the warm-up, when waiting for competition to begin, to a scene from *Star Wars – Episode I: The Phantom Menace*, where Darth Maul is battling against Jedi Master, Qui-Gon Jinn, played by Liam Neeson. The two are separated mid battle by a force field for a few minutes. Qui-Gon spends the time in meditation while Darth Maul paces like a caged tiger. Backley says:

'There's a fantastic scene where the guy with the red and black face [Darth Maul] and Liam [Qui-Gon] are in a full-on battle. Then the security bars go up and the bad guy is strutting up and down and giving up energy. Liam sits on the floor, shuts his eyes and waits. That is a nice fictitious example of the real thing in athletics where you've had the warm-up and then it's a matter of waiting and some guys are strutting up and down. It's a matter of retaining focus and how you do that is a personal thing. I go back to some of the more simple stretching routines. I have an ongoing dialogue about how I can access more potential, how I can be better. I'll go through an ankle drill exercise. I'll go through the motions of a throw, very slowly and con-trolled. After you go through the bag room and they check your bag, I go out and stretch. I have a real focus on feeling

*the stretch, feeling it going through the shoulder, across the
body, getting really in touch with the feelings and rhythms
but without expending energy.'*

During the competition, retaining focus remains key. Backley
says:

*'Your focus determines your reality. It sounds so obvious,
but it's easy to forget. In a relatively simple event – throwing
something down a field – remembering a simple phrase like
that keeps you in the present.'*

Ron Dennis, boss of the McLaren racing team, believes that
top drivers need focus if they are to be successful. Focus in
the motorsport sense is reflected in total dedication, he says.
Drivers can't be weak in any area. It's a tremendously physical sport, and they have to understand the psychological side
as well. They have to be able to withstand high cockpit tem-
peratures and dehydration. They have to be able to maintain
extreme concentration for prolonged periods. As Dennis says,
Formula One racing is not a 'burst' sport like the 100m is for
sprinters; it requires sustained concentration throughout a
lengthy race.

Dennis believes that McLaren driver David Coulthard has
the capability of winning a world championship, because he
has the discipline and focus to succeed. Dennis says:

*'Michael Schumacher once commented that he felt confi-
dent following David because he was making no mistakes
and driving so perfectly. Coulthard has the focus to win
races.'*

At the beginning of his career, golfing champion Nick Faldo was
totally focused on his golf, almost selfishly so. All he thought
about was golf. As his career developed and he became managed by IMG, Faldo enjoyed not having to worry about simple
tasks such as paying bills. That left him free to focus his mind
totally on his golf.

'They mothered me; they did everything. You went and played golf and just handed your problems to someone else. A sportsman has to have a clear head.'

Faldo didn't always find it easy to keep his concentration steady during golf competitions. In particular, when Faldo was going through divorce, he found off-course distractions multiplying around him. He says:

'At such times your mind is more cluttered and it takes a very strong mind to stay focused. To win Augusta when I was just starting to go through divorce and I had the media all over me … One of the qualities I saw then in myself was a determination not to give in just because hell's flying around. But you can only take a certain amount of that. You need an awful lot of physical and mental strength to get through it.'

Faldo remembers being totally engrossed in his shots when he won the British Open in Muirfield in 1992. During the last day he saw his lead demolished and then taken away from him, before he came back to seize the title on the eighteenth. Once he had won, he relaxed.

'If you watch, my shoulders physically drop. The adrenalin just goes wallop. I tried to stay in the same adrenalin mode off the golf course for those four days. I tried to stay in the same mental state.'

Faldo had spent the week totally involved in his golf and his attempt to win the British Open crown. He explains what that level of involvement and focus is like:

'You need someone around you who understands you and that you are quiet in the morning. You are not talking, you're thinking and you don't want them asking if you're alright. You want to be left alone because your build-up and preparation is very important. The minute you get out

of bed you're thinking about the day, replaying shots and situations.'

TASK AND PROCESS FOCUS

Sports psychologist Ian Lynagh highlights the importance for athletes of being able to maintain concentration and keep their attention focused on what they are doing. He explains that concentration relates to the broad class of being able to stay involved mentally with what you are doing. Attentional focusing is the narrow subset of that – your attention is focused on the exact little thing you need to focus on: someone is hitting a tennis ball at you at 150 miles an hour and you have to be able to see it clearly and hit it back.

What is important, Lynagh says, is task focusing – the ability to stay focusing on what you are doing and not get distracted by the score or other people or heckling. This is a difficult thing to do. It is hard to stay focused on the simplicity of swinging a golf club – even though you might be swinging it for £500,000 at that moment.

Howard Wilkinson, former Football Association technical director, agrees. He believes that aspiring champions need to learn to concentrate on the process of their particular sport – their performance – rather than on the outcome.

'There's still too much emphasis on outcome. More people can become winners if they can focus on process. It's hellish difficult, because winning – getting the gold medal or crossing the line first – is a fantastic motivator.'

Wilkinson believes that coaches and others working with sportspeople can reinforce the process aspect.

'If you're the influencing force on someone, the biggest gift you can bring is to give them the comfort, stability and consistent rationale of process and performance. Then the emotional peaks and troughs tend not to be so bad.'

Olympic rower Matthew Pinsent experiences a high sense of focus when rowing during a race, although the object of his focus can change. He pays no attention to his environment or any potential distractions.

> '*You're focusing predominantly on the techniques and the tactics of the race. Sometimes you're much more internal, focusing on technique and what you're doing to try to make the boat go quicker; and other times you're wrapped up in what the opposition are doing. But beyond those things you never think about the big race, the crowd or anything else.*'

Dr Stephanie Cook, Olympic gold medallist in modern pentathlon, had to maintain her focus over an extended competition involving five different disciplines: shooting, fencing, swimming, riding and running. In order to be successful in each separate event she had to develop the ability to direct her attention to the task in hand, and not let herself be deflected by thinking about her performance in preceding segments of the competition. Dr Cook says:

> '*In modern pentathlon, how you approach it mentally is crucial because you're not just preparing yourself for one event. The mental preparation you need for the shooting is very different from what you need for the running. Added to that, on the day of the competition, you have to deal with what's happened during the day as you go into each event. You are competing over the whole day. You might have had a good event and a very bad event and that's obviously going to affect your general mental approach. That's why you have to train mentally to be able to put whatever has happened aside and focus purely on what you're doing. You have to focus on the process, not the result. If you focus on the process, the results take care of themselves.*'

Sports psychologist Professor Graham Jones says that focusing is about keeping concentration on the present moment, and not getting distracted by past events. He says:

'It's about getting people to recognize what's happened is history. There's not a single thing they can do about it and so there's no point in worrying about it. Similarly, looking into the future is a distraction. Some golfers after 7 holes who are five under start thinking about being ten under after 18. That's as bad as being three over and thinking they're going to shoot an 81, because they're not focused on what they have to do right here and now. It's about control – what are they controlling here and now, because they need to focus on it.'

Michael Lynagh, brilliant former Australian rugby fly-half, also believes it is vital to stay focused on the immediate task at hand. He wouldn't dwell on missed kicks when he needed to be focused on the game.

'I used to put kicking in a separate box to actual play. A rugby goal kicker has to play his game regardless of how his kicking is performing. If you miss a few kicks at goal it's wrong to try and make up for it in general play. You go out and play your game. Quite regularly you see a goal kicker who misses a kick and then immediately in the next couple of plays tries to make up for it by forcing his hand; often it can lead to a downward spiral. It doesn't help his team, his performance or his goal kicking. Once you are playing, goal kicking is irrelevant until you have to goal kick. You need to be really clear what your task at hand is.

'With the kicking, you try to learn what went wrong, why you missed the last one. But you don't focus on it during play. I can remember times when I have kicked terribly, yet scored two tries and the team has won. In my mind it doesn't matter how we do it, as long as the goal is achieved in the end.'

Lynagh focused on the process, not the outcome. He says that if you concentrate on the process, the outcome will happen.

'Don't worry about the scoreboard in a rugby match. Con-centrate on each play. At the end of the day the scoreboard will look after itself. If you have played well, it will be OK. If you start concentrating on the scoreboard, protecting a lead, then your individual skills are going to fail.'

FOCUS UNDER PRESSURE

In all sports, top athletes need to keep a cool-headed focus when it counts. Modern pentathlon becomes particularly exciting when the last event arrives – the 3000m run. Competitors are given staggered starts based on their total scores so far. The person with the most points starts running before the person in second, and so on. This means that whoever wins the race has won the competition.

When Dr Stephanie Cook stepped up to the line for the race in the Sydney Olympics, she was 49 seconds behind the leader. She knew that the more people she overtook, the higher she would finish. However, she also knew that she had to run according to her own plan, and not let herself get distracted by other runners. Dr Cook says:

'I had a reputation for being a good runner. I'd always said, going into Sydney, that if I was within a minute of the leaders going into the run that I stood a good chance of running myself into a medal position.

'You have to make sure you don't get too excited about trying to beat people, and therefore lose all sense of being able to pace the race. You don't want to set off too hard in the attempt to overtake people and then burn out before you reach the end. It's a question of pacing the race completely right.

'In Sydney I knew that I had to run my own race. If you see people in front of you it gives you an added incentive to push that bit harder and overtake them, but you can't let yourself do that too early. You've got to stay in control.'

In Sydney Dr Cook managed to do this perfectly – achieving even splits throughout the race and coming home in first position to take gold.

What about when players appear to explode during a competition – shouting or storming about. Does that mean they have lost their focus? Not necessarily.

Former Davis Cup tennis captain David Lloyd accepts that it is good practice to focus on one point at a time and throw missed points out of your mind. However, he found that getting worked up could help him maintain his focus and drive.

> *'It's not good dwelling on a missed point. But I actually needed something to happen on the court. I needed to be very cross. I played better when I was cross. I needed something to excite me. I needed to think the world was against me. I liked that. It made me think "I'll do something".'*

Lloyd believes all tennis players became cross, they just didn't all show it in the same way.

> *'I'm sure Borg felt cross inside. He was just able to keep it in. I'm sure every single tennis player feels the same thing inside. It's just the way you show it. There is no way that Chris Evert didn't think, "What a f**king awful line call that was". But she didn't say it. McEnroe said it.'*

Lloyd believes a good coach needs to assess early on what approach works best for a player. If a player needs to show emotion, they should.

FOCUSING TIPS

Gazing Performance Limited, an organization specialising in mental conditioning and improving human performance, believes that controlling attention under pressure is the most important key to success. Gazing's Renzie Hanham says that one of the major keys to success lies in the deliberate focus of attention. In a stressful situation people can have negative thoughts and start acting them out. People give things labels, make judgements and then have an emotional response to them. For example, Hanham says, imagine you are competing in a multi-sport event. You are currently running up hill and the world champion runs past you. You think to yourself, 'It's the world champion!' You look at their legs and see how strong they are. You start thinking of articles you've read about them recently, how fit they're looking. You have an emotional response and start to do worse in running up the hill. You do worse because your attention is no longer on the task and your thoughts become diverted away from the task and onto such things as 'I'm not good enough ... I knew I should have trained more', and so on.

This kind of emotional response leads sportspeople into what could be called a 'negative content loop'. Their perception of what is happening triggers an emotional response that distracts their attention away from where it ought to be – on the process of what they are doing – in the above athlete's case, on the process of running up the hill. The automatic emotional response results in a poorer performance. Instead, athletes need to remain focused on the process of what they are doing, but this requires training.

The first step is to understand that such emotional responses are occurring and having an effect. Then people can start to practise observing their responses, without hooking into their emotions, Hanham says. In this way athletes can learn to separate their emotions from events and retain greater control over their attention, so remaining focused on the process.

NLP trainer Graham Shaw considers how a sportsperson can stay focused during a race or an event. He stresses the importance of awareness.

'When you are running in a road race, for example, you can be lazy; you might see something you hadn't noticed before and think, "That's interesting". But that's not going to be any good to you in the race. You need to get in the habit of asking yourself things like, "How am I running? What am

I doing now?" That way you'll automatically improve. The key thing is staying in the "now".'

But what about runners who go into an almost catatonic, trance-like state? That can happen when people become engrossed in the rhythm of their actions and are sustaining the action over a certain period of time. Shaw says:

'You will often go into that catatonic state when running or swimming or doing something like that. It connects with being in the flow zone. Yes, you can go into a trance, you can get into the flow, but if you're not periodically checking how you're doing, you almost become bereft of choice. It's different from beginning to analyse everything to the nth degree. It can be helpful to periodically check out how you're doing and make any adjustments.'

However, Shaw warns against over-analysis. This could, for example, ruin a tennis backhand or a golf swing that is working perfectly. Shaw says.

'Feel is fundamental. You could really help to screw up somebody's golf by over-analysing. Golfers who hit a really good shot say it just feels right. So you don't want to over-analyse, but you want awareness so you know when you're in the flow and when you're not.'

Former sprinter John Regis believes he suffered from over-focusing during the Barcelona Olympics in 1992:

'I was probably in the best shape of my life. In the first round I ran 20.4 seconds. Then in the second round I ran 20.2 and it was comfortable. I knew there was a monster in the tank. In the semi-final I equalled the British record. On each of these I'd been rehearsing the races the day beforehand.
'Then in the final, for some reason I'm on the blocks and suddenly my mind starts going through what I'm going to do in the race.'

Regis heard the starter say 'set', but he was still thinking about how he would run the race. Then suddenly the gun went off and he panicked.

'I just take off and I'm running like a headless chicken. For the first time since 1989 I panicked. I'm down in the race and I've got to really run. I ran the turn of my life. I ran it way too hard and then came into the home straight with nothing in the tank. I finished sixth in the Olympic final. There's no word to describe how bad I felt. Everything building up to that had been perfect. But I made the classic mistake of over-focusing.

'I haven't the foggiest idea why that happened. For this race I just decided to rerun everything in my mind. Something triggered in my mind to make sure I'd got it right. But I was absolutely gutted.'

Sports psychologist Professor Graham Jones explains that it is vital not just to focus, but to focus on the right things. Readjustment may be called for. Awareness is key. You have to be aware of when you're focusing on the wrong thing. Then you need to refocus. Professor Jones gets performers to ask themselves questions periodically, such as 'Am I focused? Am I focused on the right things?' If they are not, they need to focus on something else.

PRACTICE MAKES PERFECT

During his career, golfer Nick Faldo spent some time working with a psychologist. As a result, he learnt to stop thinking about the shots he played as simply good or bad. Instead he graded them from one to ten, with ten being the best. The psychologist would then ask Faldo what a ten shot would be. Faldo says:

'Being realistic, I'd say that a ten might end up three feet from the pole. He would say, "OK, do a 10 for me." You'd stand there and think, "Do a 10". You'd hear a shot and it

would go, plonk, three foot from the pin. I'd think, "Wow!"
I've hit some amazing shots in my career as a result of that.
That was also my first teaching about being totally focused
on your target.'

Linford Christie also improved his focus over time. When
Christie was running the 100m at the peak of his career he
always looked as if he was staring down a long tunnel. However, developing that kind of tunnel focus took him several
years. Then it just clicked, says Christie's long-time coach, Ron
Roddan. The strength of his focus could even put other athletes off. Christie's competitors would be jumping around, but
he would just stand there. His focus was plain to see.

Champion National Hunt jockey Richard Dunwoody
found that his mental preparation and ability to focus at will
improved over the course of his career.

'When I started I was mentally unprepared for a lot of rides.
But as I was doing it day in, day out, that mental prepara-
tion became stronger. I found it was easier to switch on and
off towards the end of my career. You'd go into the weighing
room and be larking around one minute, and then as soon
as you were out in the paddock, that was it – you were totally
focused on the race. You were down at the start and your
mind was on your opponents, the way your horse should
be ridden.'

Champion 400m runner Roger Black learnt during the course
of his career to focus on the things that he could control and
not worry about the rest. He sees this as being proactive, rather
than reactive.

'Most people in sport are reactive – they react to things going
on around them. All the champions I've met are proac-
tive. They don't waste any time worrying or focusing on
anything they cannot directly control. The most obvious
things to worry about are your opponents. But the reality
of a race like the 400m, where you are in separate lanes,

is that you cannot directly affect how your opponents run. You can influence them just by being there, but you can't really do anything to put them off. There is no point focusing on them.

'*For example, if you were running against someone like Michael Johnson who half-way round the track suddenly puts in a kick, then you have a choice – you either react and run with him and come last, or you don't focus on him and you do your own race.*

'*That ability to focus on the things you can control and have influence over, and not worry about things you can't control, is very important. Prior to the Atlanta Olympics the papers always talked about how hot and humid it was going to be. All athletes were talking about the weather. I didn't worry about it. I knew it was going to be hot. I knew I would have to drink fluid and I knew that was about as much as I could do. In reality, I was lucky and the four days I ran it rained. It wasn't hotter than anywhere else I had run. If I'd wasted my energy worrying about the weather it would have been a total waste of time. So it's about controlling your thoughts.*'

Modern pentathlete Dr Stephanie Cook worked hard to develop her focusing ability. She practiced mental exercises designed to improve her concentration. She could do these exercises in a variety of situations, not necessarily when actually training. One exercise involved spotting red cars when driving.

'*You start out making a really conscious effort to look out for them, and then after a while you just start seeing the red cars without concentrating on the task so much. You can translate that exercise into certain fencing moves.*

'*In another exercise we had a piece of paper with a lot of numbers written at random in a grid. You had to find each number in turn and cross it off. You had a time limit and you couldn't cross a number off until you had found the one before it.*

'These exercises were important because when competing you have to concentrate for an extended period. In pentathlon you also need to be able to broaden your focus and then bring it back to a very narrow focus for different events. You need to be able to change your range of focus and your concentration span, depending on which event you are doing. It's important to be flexible in that way in pentathlon because all the events are so diverse.'

Analysis IV

PEAK PERFORMANCE

CHAMPIONS TRAIN HARD IN ORDER TO DELIVER an unbeatable performance when it counts – on the day of competition. In Part IV we looked at how elite sportspeople manage to produce their best efforts when it really counts.

CHAPTER 12

In Chapter 12: Nerve Control, we touched on the subject of nerves – a topic with which virtually every sporting champion is familiar.

We found that even the best sportspeople suffered from nerves as competition time approached. Olympic hurdler Sally Gunnell found it hard to sleep the night before a major competition, but when she finally stood on the starting line, the foundations of self-belief that she had laid down through thorough training and preparation gave her the confidence she needed to overcome her anxieties.

Nerves shouldn't necessarily be seen as a bad thing, however. They do have value. They create adrenalin that can lift a performance.

So how did our sporting champions handle their nerves? For many, the first step was simply to accept that they would be there. England rugby fly-half Jonny Wilkinson admits to getting incredibly nervous before international and club games. He accepts this. He reads a newspaper or watches a little TV on the day of a game to keep his mind occupied. Olympic rower Matthew Pinsent says he is 'bubbling' with nerves before a race. He describes the two voices in his head – one positive and one negative. He doesn't fight these voices, but accepts that the nerves are part of the experience – part of the body's preparation for competing under stress.

Such acceptance is an appropriate response. Renzie Hanham from mental conditioning specialists Gazing Performance says that top performers accept that they need a certain level of nerves to perform at their best. People who start thinking they are too nervous risk diverting their attention away from the processes they should be concentrating on. Top performers are able to keep their attention on what they are doing, rather than being diverted into worrying about their nerves.

Being active proved helpful to some athletes in managing their pre-competition anxiety. Before a match Davis Cup tennis captain David Lloyd would hit balls on the practice court long enough to take the edge off his nerves. Former Australian rugby fly-half Michael Lynagh liked to go for a walk or kick a ball about outside his hotel in the hours before a game.

There are always exceptions in any group, and some of our interviewees did claim to have been nerve-free when competing. Former England rugby head coach Clive Woodward felt excitement rather than nerves in his playing days when a big match approached. Even without nerves, they were able to perform at the high level they required to succeed.

Applications

• Accept that you will feel nervous in certain situations. Understand that those nerves help to sharpen your performance and therefore are to be welcomed.
• Don't try to just suppress your nerves. It won't work.
• Think about situations where you handled your nerves effectively in the past. Did you do anything in particular that you could repeat in future? This could be doing something physical to let off steam or keeping your mind busy by reading a gripping book. Try to identify what works for you.

CHAPTER 13

If champions experience nerves before competition, the comfort of routine can help to keep them focused on the task in hand. In Chapter 13: The Rock of Routine, we looked at how members of the sporting elite develop and use routines to support their performance.

Successful routines are those that help to create the right mental state before a competition. Part of the value in a routine lies in the emotions with which it is associated.

Routines can develop accidentally, or deliberately with the help of sports psychologists. The aim is to identify actions that have a positive impact on the individual, arousing them to the appropriate level or generating positive mental thoughts. Once the individual knows what it is they do that has a positive impact, they can repeat that every time before competing.

The key is to identify what really works and to focus on actions that are within the individual's control, and not dependent on others. If your routine involves always wearing a pair of 'lucky' socks, then you make yourself vulnerable should you lose them. If your routine requires you to be last out on the pitch, you could have a problem if someone else in your team wants to do that too.

Renzie Hanham from mental conditioning specialists Gazing Performance encourages little rituals that people can use to control their attention – as long as they are repeatable and dependent entirely on themselves. The person must be able to control the ritual.

Champions have to be flexible enough to cope if their routine is interrupted or upset. England rugby regular Lawrence Dallaglio accepts that his routine on the day of a match has to fit around the team schedule and has to adapt to unforeseen circumstances, such as the start being delayed. Olympic rower Mathew Pinsent certainly has a warm-up routine, but beyond that tries to be as flexible as possible.

Where routines can be helpful is in creating a sense of reassuring familiarity, even if you are competing away from home or in a strange environment. Some footballers prefer playing at home, for example, because they feel they benefit from home advantage. This is partly why successful rugby kickers like former Australian rugby captain and renowned fly-half Michael Lynagh would go and kick in an unfamiliar ground the day before he was due to play there. He established a firm routine for kicking practice that helped to familiarize him with the new environment.

Applications

- Are there certain things you have done in stressful situations that have helped to keep you focused on the task in hand and not become too nervous or worked up? If so, these could become handy routines to use in similar situations. Is there a certain song you like to listen to? Are there certain images you like to picture? Do you pack your bag in a certain order to reassure yourself you haven't forgotten anything? Check that these actions and activities are within your own control and readily repeatable.

- If you have a routine you already use, think about whether it meets the repeatability and controllability criteria. If your routine is dependent on someone else or can't be repeated easily, try to find a new one.
- Look out for routines that other people use effectively. Could you learn from that routine, perhaps adapting it to meet your own needs?

CHAPTER 14

In the heat of competition, sporting champions manage to remain positive about their ability to win. In Chapter 14: Positive Talk, we looked at how they did this.

Even when in stressful competitive situations, members of the sporting elite can interpret the world and what happens to them in supportive, positive ways. Even if something happens that objectively seems bad, they can turn it around into a positive opportunity.

The ability to do this depends on the language that people use when thinking or speaking to themselves. For example, a triathlete could interpret the pain he felt in competition as a wonderful indicator that he was alive.

Some techniques for keeping a positive outlook are extremely simple. Just standing in a confident way will make you feel more confident. Modern pentathlete Dr Stephanie Cook appreciated this; she focused on keeping her body language positive and walking tall even when her fencing wasn't going as well as she would like. Champions also accept that sometimes their performance can slip, but if they just hang in there and stay in the competition, they give themselves a chance of coming back.

Just thinking about what you need to do at any one moment is also a good technique for warding off negative thoughts and staying in a positive space. Similarly, focusing your attention within yourself, and not watching what others are doing, can also support positive feelings. Former sprinter John Regis made a point of not watching others warming up because in the past he found it made him worry about how good his rivals looked. Olympic hurdler Sally Gunnell maintained a strong sense of calm and focus when she was waiting in the call room before racing. She sensed she gave off such a strong aura that it put her competitors off.

Champions can try to psyche each other out, unconsciously or consciously. Linford Christie, 100m champion, seemed to put other people off just by being in close proximity to them; his sense of belief was almost tangible. However, he could also deliberately psyche rivals out if he was so minded – warming up in someone else's lane.

Ceri Evans from mental conditioning specialists Gazing Performance accepts that in competition, athletes or players often try to put each other off by disturbing their focus. Such tricks are designed to divert the other people away from focusing on their own processes. If you find yourself on the receiving end, it is important to continue to place your attention on the things that you can control or influence.

Renzie Hanham from Gazing Performance explains that diverting from process can be harmful to performance because it is often accompanied by an internal dialogue which has to do with whether you can perform or not. One part of you says 'you can' and one part says 'you can't'. Inevitably this impacts negatively on the quality of your processes because your attention is divided. The physical results of this internal dilemma are feelings of heaviness, lethargy and a drop-off in co-ordination. The psychological results are doubt and uncertainty, which lead to poor decision-making. Because we are not sure we can trust ourselves, our thinking is inaccurate. We lose our confidence.

Conversely, Hanham explains, when we are totally in process and on task there is only the thought 'I do'. There is only certainty, an inner stillness and a conviction that you are in the right place at the right time. You are, as some people call it, 'in the zone' – a state we considered further in Chapter 15.

Applications

- Make use of simple physical techniques – such as standing confidently – that can encourage you to think positively.
- Pay attention to the language you use when talking to yourself mentally. Do you tend to use a critical internal voice? If so, try to speak to yourself in more encouraging tones, which emphasize the positive aspects of situations or events.
- If you know you will face a situation that tends to put you in a negative frame of mind, think in advance about how you can describe it to yourself differently. For example, you may be feeling anxious about going through an assessment process for a new job. You are worried that the assessment exercises will highlight your weaknesses in report writing. Instead, think about how you will be able to show your strengths in team-building and communication. Focus on how the experience should generate valuable feedback to help you develop your skills. It is a great opportunity to learn about yourself. Do you feel more excited about the experience now?
- Get into the habit of asking yourself what process you should be focusing on right now. This helps to stop you getting diverted by emotional responses to events.
- If someone else is trying to put you off, don't pay attention to them. Remind yourself that it is what you are doing that counts.

CHAPTER 15

When sportspeople deliver their best performances, they often talk about having been 'in the zone'. In Chapter 15: Into the Zone, we looked at what the sporting elite means by this and how they try to get into that state when they need it.

When sportspeople get into the zone, what they do feels effortless. Former sprinter Mark Richardson describes the sensation of time slowing down and being able to see everything clearly. Olympic hurdler Sally Gunnell says she felt she went into automatic pilot, so much so that she couldn't remember what happened in the race once it was over. This is not unusual. Athletes can become so in tune with what they are doing that they have no recollection of what they actually did or how they did it.

Renzie Hanham from mental conditioning specialists Gazing Performance stresses that for all of us, 'there is only now'. In real terms as we experience life, there is only one point in time available to us – the present moment. Whether we are reflecting on the past or planning for the future, we can only do this 'now'. This is an important point, Hanham says, because much of our attention is unconsciously diverted by things past and future. When we are under pressure we start to identify with past or future events as if they were happening in the present moment. This distorts our perception and filters the way that we respond to events. Clear thinking becomes lost as we revert to familiar patterns of behaviour – what we are comfortable with.

When athletes speak of being 'in the zone', they are operating in the 'now'. There is just no room for doubt because doubt is of the future. Being in the zone happens when you are totally on task and in process. There is no room for diversions. That doesn't mean you are blank – far from it. You are still receiving information and that information is being digested accurately and efficiently and adds to the quality of your process.

Hanham suggests that it is useful to practise staying present when reflecting on the past or planning for the future. One way of achieving this is by staying aware of your body, i.e. your breathing. This simple technique stops you from identifying so strongly with your thoughts that you start responding as if the thoughts were real, as opposed to just thoughts. The prime issue here is control of attention and being deliberate about where you place your attention.

Getting into the zone is no easy matter. Most interviewees admitted they had no guaranteed method for doing so. The state might be associated with certain emotions, such as confidence and belief, but there were no guarantees that these would lead them into the zone.

For javelin champion Steve Backley, the zone was like entering a 'superstate' – an experience he first enjoyed in 1990 when he came from behind to win an international competition, achieving a new British record in the process. In the experience, Backley felt dissociated – it was as if he was watching himself making the throw from two or three feet away, rather than actually doing it himself.

From that time Backley worked hard to try to recreate the superstate at will, doing so by asking himself questions about his performance – a form of self-analysis. He developed theories about it, such as that lots of sleep was required in advance of competition. He also noted that the superstate seemed to be created out of adversity, as a result of extreme anxiety or pressure.

While athletes may strive to achieve such a superstate or enter the zone, they need to guard against becoming obsessive about it. Ceri Evans from Gazing Performance says that concentrating too hard on trying to get back into the zone, or indeed whether they are in the zone or out of it, can be a diversion that actually impedes performance. If they focus on how to get back into the zone, they can be diverted from focusing on the process of what they are doing. The important thing is to continue to focus purely on effective process. Whether someone is in or out of the 'zone' is an outcome of this heightened concentration. For most athletes, it occurs infrequently during their careers. It may be more helpful not to see it as an 'all or none' phenomenon. In this way, the athlete can concentrate on just improving their focus of attention, something they do have control over, rather than whether they are in the zone or not, which may or may not occur. Concerning oneself with things that have happened in the past and potential negative outcomes in the future weakens the connection or engagement with the present, and makes entering the 'zone' more unlikely.

Applications

- Being 'in the zone' can be useful for anyone who wants to be totally engaged in what they are doing.
- Think about occasions in the past when you felt 'in the zone' or 'in the now'. Was there anything particular that you did to achieve that? Is there anything you could try to repeat in future?
- Don't get too hung up on the outcome – the zone – at the expense of the processes involved in what you are doing. You want to keep your attention focused on the processes that you are completing now.

CHAPTER 16

In Chapter 16: Focus and Refocus, we looked at how sporting champions manage to retain their focus during competition.

Focus is all about keeping your mind and your attention on the task in hand – not what is going on around you. This isn't easy. Even sporting legends such as Nick Faldo could struggle to remain totally concentrated on their sport when their personal lives hit problems. However, at its best, Faldo's focus was impressive. From the moment he woke on the day of play he was preparing himself internally and thinking about the day ahead.

During competition, the key is to retain focused on the task or the process involved at any particular time. During a race Olympic rower Matthew Pinsent, for example, would never let his focus stray to thinking about the crowd or the importance of the occasion. He mainly focused on the technique of rowing. Modern pentathlete Dr Stephanie Cook didn't let herself get distracted when running in her last event at the Sydney Olympics. She stuck to her race plan, regardless of those around her.

Being focused involves staying in the present moment, and not letting past events distract you. This means poor previous performances, shots and missed kicks must all be set aside.

Nor is it wise to start thinking about the future, and what may happen later in a match or game.

The sporting champions we interviewed understood the importance of being able to segment their performances, depending on what they were doing. Former Australian rugby fly-half Michael Lynagh would concentrate on kicking when he was kicking, then focus on the rest of the game during open play. If he was performing badly in one area of his game, he didn't let himself dwell on it when performing in another area. Nor would he think about the scoreboard, but simply about each play as it happened. His ability to retain strong focus, even when under extreme pressure, enabled him to snatch wins in the closing minutes of games.

However, some champions also described occasions when they felt they had 'over-focused'. At the last minute they began thinking in too great detail about what they were about to do. There is a balance to be struck between thinking about each element of a tennis shot or a golf swing and focusing on the familiar feel of what you do. This can actually destroy performance by disrupting the flow.

Ceri Evans from mental conditioning specialists Gazing Performance says that despite being a remarkably complex organ, one of the main constraints on brain functioning is that humans have a limited ability to focus on more than one thing at a time, particularly under conditions of pressure. With a golf swing, for example, professional golfers will actually focus on very few things. They won't think about every element involved in the swing because this would be likely to cause mechanical breakdown, or paralysis by analysis. They need first to have over-learned the skill. This means that the basic mechanics are firmly enough established that they don't need to think consciously about every element of the swing as they do it. They may then focus on the feel of the swing, rather than multiple technical elements.

Practice is important when working to develop good focus. The champions we interviewed learnt over time what preparations and techniques helped to maintain their focus.

Dr Stephanie Cook completed mental exercises designed to improve her concentration and focus.

Experience also taught the athletes the importance of not getting distracted by things beyond their control. Champion 400m runner Roger Black learnt that worrying about the weather during the Atlanta Olympics would only be a waste of energy.

Maintaining strong focus is a skill. Champions need to learn that emotional responses to events around them distract them from what they are doing. Ceri Evans from Gazing Performance says that some champions learn not to attach emotive labels to people or circumstances. Instead they observe calmly. In this way they can keep their attention on the process of what they are doing. This detached viewpoint can help to retain focus, without unhelpful emotions generated by labelling and judging getting in the way.

Applications

- If you want to develop a greater sense of focus, develop the habit of asking yourself periodically what you are focusing on. If you are not focusing on the process of what you are currently doing, gently bring your attention back to the process.
- Understand that past and future events are not relevant to what you are doing right now. If you find yourself dwelling on a mistake you made last time you were in your current position, bring your mind back to the process of what you are doing now.
- If you find you need to focus on several different things at different times, be clear about what is most important now. Segment what you do into separate chunks of activity. Whichever activity you are doing now, make that the focus of your attention.
- Don't waste time focusing your attention on things you cannot control.

- Practise observing events without becoming emotionally involved. Focus your attention on what is happening, rather than on attaching emotive and emotional descriptors.
- If you want to improve your concentration, play games that can help to train your mind appropriately.

Part V
TEAM SPIRIT

Chapter 17

THE RIGHT COMBINATION

IN MANY SPORTS NO ONE INDIVIDUAL can ensure a win. It is the team effort that counts. Putting together the right combination of individuals is therefore critical for the overall success of the team – and everyone in it.

TEAM SELECTION

When choosing players for the team, England manager Sven-Göran Eriksson aims to try and create an overall positive chemistry. He says:

> 'It can happen that you don't select players who you know may not fit in with the group, even if they are very good players. You put in players who you know will give you

something, even if they are sitting on the bench. They create a good atmosphere, are positive and support the eleven who are playing. That's extremely important, especially when you are competing away in a World Cup.'

Jack Charlton was selected to play for England relatively late in the day. He believes that Alf Ramsay, despite selecting him, didn't like him. However, Charlton was included in the team because he fitted the desired pattern of play. Charlton recalls:

'I was 28 coming up 29 when I got my first cap. I asked Alf, "Why me?" He said, "Well Jack, I have a pattern of play in my mind – the way I want the team to play. So I always pick appropriate players to make the pattern work. I don't necessarily always pick the best players, Jack."'

Charlton absorbed this information and used it himself when he was a manager. He understood that as a national team manager he had to start with a desired way or pattern of playing. Then he had to select the players who would be able to make that pattern work. He couldn't just pick people for the team because they had talent.

THE CAPTAIN

Selecting the captain is particularly important in putting together the right combination of players in a successful team. England manager Sven-Göran Eriksson is impressed by David Beckham's qualities as captain. He appreciates the fact that Beckham doesn't shout, but just by his behaviour on and off the pitch, the other players follow him, listen to him and respect him.

In the match between England and Greece in 2001, Beckham took the extra time free kick which assured England's qualification for the 2002 World Cup. This is just one example of the mental strength that Beckham has shown on many occasions. Eriksson says:

'Even his World Cup penalty against Argentina wasn't easy. Any player could easily see the goal as being very small and the goalkeeper as very big, because all the nation is watching and this is an opportunity to score.'

Michael Lynagh was captain of Australia from 1992 to 1995. He recalls his experiences of having that role, and the differences between himself and his predecessor, Nick Farr-Jones. Lynagh says:

'I enjoyed the responsibility. I had been captain of school teams in both cricket and rugby and various teams in Queensland. My one problem was that I am a fairly quiet and reserved person. As captain you do have to make an effort to be heard and have points of view and talk to people. Nick Farr-Jones was very good at that; he was a very outgoing and personable person and that is why I thought we made such a good team when he was captain and I was vice captain. I looked after everything behind him on the pitch and he looked after everything in front of him. Off the pitch we were very good friends but had very different personalities. In a way we complimented one another very well.

'When Nick retired and I took over, I had to reinvent myself a little bit. But if I stood in the dressing room and started thumping the table and swearing at the forwards and saying "Come on, you have got to do this and that", they wouldn't have taken me seriously because they knew that wasn't me. Part of captaincy is delegating to people who are in a position to do that, and that is what I did. I got people within the team who were experienced as my deputies. They weren't necessarily vice captains but they were leaders of men within that team and within groups of that team. That is how I overcame my shyness in terms of being a captain. I could look after the backs, because I had done that for many years. With the forwards, I got key people within the forwards to look after them – to stir them up and do what forwards do.

> *'So I delegated, but I also became more assertive in terms of team meetings. Before I was captain I was quite happy to listen and work things out later, but now I had to lead meetings and that was quite a change of direction for me.'*

Despite his enjoyment of the captain's role, Lynagh tried not to forget that the success of the team was more important than his own personal glory. Lynagh says:

> *'The team has always been very important to me. My personal goal was always to try and get the team to play better. I was disappointed when I missed out on being captain on a few occasions, but at the end of the day if I was in the team – terrific.*
>
> *'At Saracens there was an occasion when someone was dropped as captain and he moped around and didn't perform. I hadn't agreed with the decision to drop him as captain, but when I saw his reaction I knew it was the right decision. I thought he was the wrong person to be captain because he was putting himself before the team. He wasn't the right person to lead because he thought about himself before the team.'*

TEAM SPIRIT

Team spirit comes from a general recognition amongst all team members that the good of the team comes before the needs of the individual. Roger Black recalls how the British 4 × 400m relay team beat the Americans in the 1991 World Championships.

> *'On paper, we were not capable of winning the gold medal, but we had a shared belief – that the greater good of the team was more important than any individual ego. That is the secret of teamwork. The 1991 British 4×400 team was myself – an individual silver medallist in the 400m, Derek Redmond, who was the British 400m record holder and who was coming back from an injury, John Regis, a*

*200m runner, and Kriss Akabusi, the bronze medallist in
the 400m hurdles.*

*'We won the 1991 gold because of something that hap-
pened the night before the race. Choosing the running order
wasn't difficult. You would generally put the best athlete on
the last leg and an OK athlete on the first leg and the other
two in the middle.'*

The original chosen running order was therefore Redmond
first, Akabusi second, Regis third and Black fourth. However,
the night before the race Black and Akabusi decided they
needed to change the order. Black says:

*'We had chosen the right team, but the right team for second
place. Sometimes in sport you have to dare to win. You have
to take an opportunity. We knew we weren't doing that. We
had to become proactive as a team and make the Americans react to us, which they would never do with this order.
They would go from the front and be in the lead. Off they
would go and win. We had to change that. We had to make
the Americans think before they even walked into the stadium.'*

The team decided they needed to surprise the Americans by
putting Black on the first leg, followed by Redmond and Regis,
with Akabusi on the last leg. Black says:

*'We knew that was our only chance. It was a risk – a big
risk. We called an emergency meeting with the team management and said we wanted to change the running order.
I will never forget their faces. It took about half an hour
of intelligent discussion. One of the team managers said
something, which I think is a great example of good management, which was, "In the end you are the four guys who
have to run. We will be sitting in the stands watching you. If
you really believe in each other as a team, you must do this."
So we shaped our destiny.'*

Black recalls the impact that the new, unexpected order had on the Americans. When the British team went and sat on the benches before the race in their revised order, the US team members were extremely surprised. Black says:

'Before you go out into the stadium you have to sit in the order you are going to run in; and when I went and sat on the first bench, we "had" the Americans. All they had been thinking about was how fast they were going to run, and they had been arguing about who was going to run the last leg.'

The Americans were shocked because the fastest runner always ran the last leg and never the first. There were various reasons, as Black explains:

'When you are the fastest runner in the team and you are the world's silver medallist, you don't expect to run the first leg. It had never been done for three reasons. Firstly, because you look rubbish because you run in lanes; secondly, you get the slowest time of the team. Thirdly, if the team happens to win you don't get your picture in the paper. The guy on the last leg gets all the glory.'

However, the four British athletes decided to put their egos aside. Black says:

'I was very happy to do that. We all were. The Americans weren't. When we walked out into the stadium the four of us didn't have to talk to each other at all; we had the Americans beat because they were going, "Wow, what's he doing first? What's going to happen?" They were being reactive and we were being proactive.

'That night when I stood behind the line to run that first leg, I wasn't running for myself, I wasn't running for Great Britain. I was actually running for John Regis, Derek Redmond and Kriss Akabussi. That to me was a moment of absolute perfection of teamwork. It was truly amazing

because what was interesting was that Kriss Akabussi didn't choose to run the last leg because he wanted personal glory; he did what I think many people wouldn't have done. He put himself under a lot of pressure. Of course, he got all the credit and all the glory, but you put your ego to one side for the greater good of the team.

'That to me was such a wonderful moment because individual success is great but you can't really share it with anybody. When the four of us get together we still reminisce. We have got that bond for the rest of our lives.'

The Australian 1991 World Cup rugby team was an impressive one, former captain Michael Lynagh believes, because of the players within it and the strong team ethos. The team included an older, experienced core of people who were probably at the peak of their powers. Then there was also a young group, whose talents were enormous and who were very easy to mould into a team. Lynagh recalls:

'We all got on very well. There was a good vibe in the team. We enjoyed each other's company away from rugby. Our wives were friendly with one another. But we were winning, so there weren't many problems to have to deal with.

'There were certain values in the team, certain standards that were set, ways you were expected to behave. It was very much a self-governed operation, but there were rules.

'Discipline came from within the team. If somebody was out of line it wouldn't be the manager or coach who came down on them; one of the guys in the team would quietly have a word.'

SUPPORT TEAMS

In motorsport, the team around the driver is vital for success. Ron Dennis, boss of the McLaren racing team, knows the importance of getting the mix right. Some teams give guidance and support, he says, and some don't. The environment in McLaren helps to support the driver, and the team includes people who are experts in a range of different areas. They can give advice, for example, on issues not directly associated with the motor racing itself, such as how to handle adverse publicity.

McLaren driver David Coulthard benefited from the McLaren support after he survived a traumatic plane crash, and drove in a race just days later. Dennis says:

> *'I have tremendous admiration for him, but also personal pride in how we reacted and shielded him from the media to enable him to collect his thoughts. I was proud of the role of the team, and my contribution to it.'*

Even in normal circumstances, the team needs to work in a unified, focused way to deliver success on the track. As Dennis says:

> *'You constantly have to define the goal, and the role that everyone has to play to achieve it. It's like a chain. You have to make sure that everyone understands they have a role to play, and that they can make a difference. It's like in football where there are also so many people behind the scenes. Everyone has to be of a mindset where they know they can make a difference, including the guy checking the studs to make sure that none are loose.*
>
> *'These cars are complex animals. You get a great sense of achievement from getting them off the line and surviving the first lap. The driver is an ingredient – an important one – but an ingredient in the makeup. No driver has won a Grand Prix from sitting at the start line in his underpants.'*

That said, the driver is a central element. On race day, the driver takes centre stage. Dennis says:

> *'The driver is one element of the team and he becomes the focus of everyone's efforts at a Grand Prix. There are various points where you feel yourself thinking, "Now it's over to him".'*

Once teams are selected, their members still need to function well together to achieve consistent winning performances. In the next chapter we look at how top sportspeople work together to achieve a great team performance at the right time.

Chapter 18

TEAM BUILD-UP

BUILDING A STRONG TEAM TAKES TIME and commitment from all those involved – team members, managers, coaches and support staff.

TEAM VALUES

Sports psychologist and performance expert Professor Graham Jones knows that team members need to buy into a common set of values if the team is to become strong and successful. Those values are important in terms of the way the team does things, and the things that are acceptable. Professor Jones has worked with teams on developing team charters and has encouraged them to police themselves. He feels it is important to empower the team to determine what happens if someone contravenes the charter. That empowerment encourages the development of a strong team spirit. Professor Jones says:

> *'You recognize and accept that you are all part of the same team. You develop a common vision, so that you are all working towards the same thing. You accept that people are different. There may be different levels of skill, but everyone has something to contribute to the team.'*

In addition to team values, strong teams require a culture where it is OK to make mistakes, says Renzie Hanham from Gazing Performance, specialists in performance improvement. Strong teams have a culture of looking after people and keeping them safe and secure. Trust is very important. In dysfunctional teams, if someone makes a mistake, they pay for it. Team members identify themselves as being challenged all the time and that becomes counter-productive. They see a criticism as a threat. Hanham adds that team spirit arises out of good or useful shared experiences, such as enjoyment or good performances. People that are winning are generally happy.

NLP trainer Graham Shaw believes that developing a supportive culture is important in terms of training players not to panic in tough match moments. Teams can learn how to cope when things go wrong in competition. He recalls the England–Brazil match in the 2002 World Cup.

> *'When Brazil scored, while it was a terrible time to let a goal in, I think the match was totally lost then. I don't think it was down to David Seaman. As a team, one of the things that's important is what happens when things begin to go wrong. If we let a goal in, what are the things we are going to say to each other and do and how are we going to hold our heads?*
>
> *'It's interesting that when Arsene Wenger is interviewed after a match he focuses on talking about the performance. He doesn't get too carried away if he's won. If he's lost 1–0, he knows that from time to time you perform well but let a*

goal in and lose. He knows, however, that over time if they
perform well they'll win.

'How many times have Manchester United scored a goal
near the end of a match? How do they do that? They don't
do that by panicking. What they do is say, "We know that
most of the time, if we continue to play in this way, we'll
score".'

Shaw says that a team can prepare in advance for adverse situations. Team members can be encouraged to think in advance about how they will react should the opposition score. In effect, they need to learn to keep their heads up, to avoid wasting time on blaming someone and to get straight on with the match.

Howard Wilkinson, former Football Association technical director, believes in the importance of getting every player to buy into the team's objectives and the process for achieving them.

'Get their agreement, get them to buy into it, and then use
that as the reference point. Show them you're prepared to
take the giant step; show them you're prepared to be inno-
vative; show them that the goal can be achieved. But take
the fear out of it by showing them how you're going to get
there, by breaking it down into things to concentrate on in
the short-term, and what you can affect in the long-term,
and why and how.'

Wilkinson doesn't believe there are any tricks or gimmicks that can really create team spirit.

'I've tried them, and they weren't for me. I've always thought
it is more about having agreed objectives with everybody
buying into them. It's about having an identifiable coat of
arms or trademark for the way we do things here; making
certain values important and emphasizing them all the
time: respect, trust, being fair, sharing, doing your best.'

TEAM COMMUNICATION

Sports psychiatrist John Syer believes that effective communication is vital for developing team spirit. Syer and his
colleagues employ a model derived from Gestalt Therapy to
define a team building approach. Syer says:

> *'Initially team members must become aware of themselves.
> If I don't know what I'm doing when I'm with my team,
> I'm not going to perform very well. I also need to be aware
> of other team members: what impact I have on them, how
> they are different to myself and how they are different to
> each other. Then I come to appreciate those differences
> – not necessarily to like them – but to appreciate that this
> player needs to do this in order to perform well and I must
> find a way to allow him to do this.*
>
> *'The heart of the process is giving descriptive feedback
> to each other about what they see happening, what they see
> each other doing, what they see happening as a result and
> how they feel. It's not what they think, but how they feel –
> expressed in one word – that counts. We call this descriptive
> feedback, whereas the normal type of feedback is evaluative
> and is concerned to congratulate or criticize.*
>
> *'When we're working with a team, we focus on what
> people are doing and help members to report their experi-
> ences. By making feedback descriptive, comments between
> team members arouse interest rather than defensiveness.'*

Syer suggests that team members communicate how their
performance is helped or hindered by the performance of
other team members. This kind of information is rarely given.
Yet Syer says that if you always give descriptive feedback and
appreciation, then you get all the things that the team needs:
contact, communication, respect, trust, team spirit.

The exact team-building exercises that Syer would go
through with a particular team would depend on the particular
circumstances. However, the exercise itself is not important.

What is important, Syer says, is that you facilitate people talking to each other in a way they understand. He says:

'We have to speak to make contact. The skills of communication are central to this. But exactly what I do depends on the particular team. In fact I always start by meeting each member of the team individually. That's because everyone's experience of what is going on at a given moment is slightly different. We notice different things. With a team, it's important that people have the chance to express their own reality.'

Team communication was an important element of the build-up to one of Blyth's team sailing challenges. To encourage team spirit, Blyth took his group of sailors to Scotland.

'I took them up to a small cottage in Scotland for three weeks. I'd written a training programme and for three weeks there were 25 of us in a cottage with only two bedrooms upstairs and a sitting room. We lay on army camp beds. We simulated conditions on a boat so they had to make their beds up and keep the place clean and tidy. We went for a run every morning. We had discipline. We had discussions chaired by one of the guys. We'd break into watches. We did various activities so we had to work as a team.'

TEAM BUILD-UP

Lawrence Dallagio, England rugby captain, knows that his success as an England player depends on the achievements of other team members. He says:

'We have an expression in rugby that you have to look after your own back yard. If everyone in the team does that, and everyone is pulling in the right direction, then you get the result you want. Ultimately, because it's a technical game, you are relying on other people's performances for you to succeed.'

The difficult part, however, is to try and ensure that everyone performs well at the same time. As Dallaglio says, in a team game you have to get all the components to be at the right level at the same time. If an individual is mentally stronger than his opponent and he's physically better, then he's going to win. But in a team game, if three or four players turn up and play well but the others don't, it's very difficult. The mechanics of team sport involve trying to get the best out of everyone at the same time. If you do that, you get a perfect performance.

In the week before a game, preparations include analysing the opposition.

'You look at what you are going to do, and you look at what the opposition are going to do and how you are going to stop that. There is part of the week where you have to pay respect to the opposition, analyse their weaknesses and strengths and work out strategies to counteract them. You have to work out technically how you as an individual, and as a team, are going to overcome the opposition's strengths – your game plan. There's a fair bit of mental work that goes into that. The closer I get to a game, the more I start to think about the team I'm playing against. I start to picture the opposition. I start to visualize them. I put myself in the game environment and atmosphere, so that you're not there for the first time when the whistle blows; you've already been there and you know what to expect.'

Individuals playing sport as part of a team need to be sensitive to the needs of the team when preparing to compete. As Dallagio knows, they can't just expect to follow a routine that works for them. Individual routines have got to be flexible. Individual performers can have much more influence over what happens, but as a team player, Dallaglio says, sometimes you've got to give a little bit for the sake of the team. That may mean making adjustments in terms of your own preparation.

Ron Dennis, boss of the McLaren racing team, understands the challenges involved in keeping a team motivated. He believes it is easier to motivate people when things are not going so well than it is when they are enjoying a period of success. In fact, he says, motivating people who are successful is the most difficult thing to have to do.

Dennis likens a team to a flywheel, fuelled by the energy that comes from the desire to win.

'It slowly gets up speed and reaches the speed needed for success. And you start to succeed. Then suddenly something happens – perhaps the technical or team manager retires or you lose one of your drivers – but you still win. What happens though is that there is a dropping down of energy input into the flywheel. When you start to fail it's after a sustained period of lack of effort. And it takes time to build the whole thing back up again.'

In other words, the biggest enemy of continuous success is continuous success.

EXTENDED TOURNAMENTS

During competitions such as the football World Cup, players have to be able to handle living together away from home for extended periods. It is important to create a harmonious team spirit, as England manager Sven-Göran Eriksson knows.

'That's very important and very difficult. It depends on the results you are achieving; the best medicine for having a good ambience is winning football games. You can never beat that. But when you are together for such a long time it's important that you are not only practising, eating and sleeping; you have to do other things too. You can go and play golf, or out fishing. Sometimes we go to dinner in other restaurants. You have to create events, otherwise it will be very boring.'

After the 2002 World Cup Eriksson asked his players for feedback on certain aspects of the team organization, to see whether there was anything that could be done differently next time to help them. For example, Eriksson wondered whether the team would rather move around different locations, rather than always travelling to and from the same base camp for matches which resulted in some long journeys. The feedback was that players liked to stay in the base camp, because that became their home from home. Having such a base gave players a sense of familiarity with their surroundings and added security.

Security and confidence are also boosted when schedules run to time. Eriksson explains:

'In a football team, it's important to know exactly when you will be leaving your hotel and arriving at the stadium. You want to arrive there exactly at the right time – not two hours before, not one hour before, but one hour twenty minutes before. Sometimes things happen – there's traffic or the police escorting the bus are too slow. But it's important to arrive at the right time, because if you have too much time, you don't know what to do with it. If you have too little, then you are rushing too much. I actually think it's better to have less time than more time, because you don't know what to do in the dressing room if you have too much time; you lose concentration.'

Howard Wilkinson, former Football Association technical manager, knows that mental fitness is important for coping well with protracted tournaments. Wilkinson says:

'A big part of tournament football is about R&R – mentally and physically. It's very important. In the last World Cup, England were away for six weeks. If they had gone to the finals they would probably have been away for seven and a half weeks. That's very unusual for football.

'And with international tournament football, you're in a hotel and because of the high profile, you're unlikely to go exploring the streets.'

So apart from coping with the physical challenges of playing in a different climate or adjusting to a new time zone, top players also need to be able to cope with boredom. They need to be able to handle going from a very active state into a very low gear.

STRATEGIC PLANNING

Strategic planning in a team situation so that everyone knows what they need to do is essential for sporting success. Former Ireland manager Jack Charlton stresses the importance of having a pre-agreed pattern of play. He says everyone thinks that if you've got eleven of the best players in the world, you would automatically beat everybody. Unfortunately, that's not the case. The team members have to work together, Charlton says. They have got to fit into some sort of pattern, because without that they have nothing – no intent, and no knowledge of where to play the ball.

As Charlton explained in the previous chapter, he selected players who suited the pattern of play he wanted to develop. That pattern of play could vary, however.

> *'With the Irish team I designed a game I called "putting them under pressure". FIFA decided they would call it "pressing". You played the ball behind people, but instead of just letting two forwards chase, everybody followed the ball and pushed in. We didn't let people out of their half. We had great success with that game once the players understood what was necessary.'*

Charlton also believes it is better to give players one simple instruction, rather than a choice of options. It is better to tell a player to knock the ball behind the fullback every time he gets it than suggest a choice of actions.

> *'The more you complicate the methods of playing, the more difficult they are to get through to the players and the longer*

*it takes them to accept what you say. Normally by that time
you will have got the sack!'*

One of Charlton's great strategic successes in terms of developing a new pattern of play came at Middlesborough, the first club he managed after leaving Leeds United in 1973. When Charlton arrived the side had a problem getting caught offside when attacking. Charlton devised a solution whereby a midfield runner, Alan Foggon, would hold himself deep onside and then chase after balls played forward behind the defence. The key for the move to work, however, was that the two forwards had to run back faster than the defence who were trying to use the offside rule. Charlton says:

> *'They had to remember to get out quicker than the defenders and not turn and chase a ball when they were offside. Now you think it's easy to tell people something and get them to do it. It's not easy. It took six months before I could get the two forward players both feeding off to an onside position instead of staying in an offside position. It took six months to get it through to them. But when they grabbed it, we murdered the division.*
>
> *'Foggy did it remarkably well. The moment he had got through, everybody turned round and raced back. The number of times that Foggy used to stand on the ball or slide along the ground on his face and put the ball over the bar – but it didn't matter. We won the Second Division Championship by 15 or 20 points. We got promoted into the First Division in my first year through a method and way of playing.'*

Charlton claims the game that gave him greatest satisfaction was when Ireland, which he was managing, played Brazil in Dublin. Part of his satisfaction came from the fact that Liam Brady performed his role perfectly. Charlton says:

> *'I had been trying to get through to Liam how I wanted him to play. I told him I didn't want him playing off the back*

four, but off the front two, so he was playing in midfield and getting close to people up front.

'Liam that day was brilliant. We beat Brazil 1–0 and Liam scored the winning goal. Liam looked as though he was going to cross the ball to the far post. Everybody reacted and the goalkeeper went across to the far post. Then Liam struck the ball straight in the bottom corner on the other side of the goal. It was because he was in a position that the opposition didn't like and I felt that I had been responsible in some way for getting Liam into that position. With Arsenal, Liam would take the ball off the back four and play it through midfield. I didn't want him doing that. I wanted him taking it off the front two and then playing from there.'

Charlton also appreciates the value of attention to detail when preparing for matches, a lesson he learnt when playing for Leeds United. Leeds' manager Don Revie put huge effort into his briefings, seemingly knowing about all the players in every opposition team. Charlton says:

'After lunch we would sit down with Don for half or three quarters of an hour while Don went through his notes. He itemized every player – how they played, where they played the ball, whether they were good, whether they were quick. He knew every player in the Football League better than they knew themselves. It was called attention to detail. We knew where they would cause us problems. After the first six months we would fall asleep and he would start yelling at us. He would yell, "We've spent bloody hours chasing round all over this country to get information to give to you that will win you the game tomorrow if you listen. Don't you fall asleep on me!"'

Team briefings aren't only important during team practice. They come into their own in the closing stages before a competition, and particularly just before a match. In the next chapter we look at how team captains, coaches and managers brief their teams just before, and during, competitive games.

Chapter 19

TEAM TALKS

WHAT HAPPENS IN THE LAST MINUTES before a team goes out to compete? In this chapter we consider the most successful changing-room routines for encouraging a top class performance.

THE CAPTAIN'S ROLE

The captain plays an important role in helping to create a positive team state before a competition. Michael Lynagh, former Australia rugby captain, was generally pretty quiet before matches.

> 'When I was captain I would walk around in the dressing room and talk a bit, see that everybody was alright. I would

get people together to ensure everybody was ready. Even when I wasn't captain, as a leader in the team, that was still my role.

'When I was captain sometimes some of the forwards needed a firm voice. If I started banging the table they would realize something was up. I was never really loud. I used to get other people to do that for me. I made sure the vice captain and so on knew what they were doing.'

Lynagh didn't find he needed to spend much time on motivating the Australian team.

'When you are dealing with guys who are fairly elite sportsmen you don't really need to motivate them. They were very self-motivated. Before a game it was more about pointing the herd in the right direction and bringing all that individual motivation together. I used to do that in a different way to Nick Farr-Jones, who was captain before me. Nick was quite an orator; he would stand up and away he would go.

'In contrast, I would go and spend time with individual people within the team. I would make the effort to go and have breakfast with somebody and then have lunch with somebody else and go and have a cup of coffee in the afternoon with somebody else. That took me out of my comfort zone. I used to have guys who I was comfortable with and would spend a lot of time with. But instead of playing golf in the afternoon with my regular mates I would make an effort to go and talk to people like Garrick [Morgan], which was great fun. I would have to do that, to see how they were feeling and if they were happy. That was important to me because if you are not happy, your motivation wanes.

'The guys could see that I was doing this, and that I was trying, and they reacted accordingly. So there was good feedback for me. That is how I ran the team.'

David Lloyd, former Davis Cup tennis captain, believes that individual team members need to be treated differently, according to their own personalities and styles of play. The key to a good Davis Cup captain, he says, is to get inside the players' minds because they are all very different. Lloyd says:

> 'People used to ask me why I didn't talk to Tim Henman on court, but there isn't any reason to talk to Tim on court. He doesn't want to be spoken to. If you speak to him he gets pissed off and doesn't play. With Greg Rusedski, you can't get him hyped up. Some people you have to rev up, and some people you've got to keep in low gear.
>
> 'With Tim, you don't really have to do anything. He goes into a slight trance and then you just leave him. You know he's going to get out there and win. If he's got a problem, he'll ask you.'

PRE-MATCH TALKS

On match day, coaches and managers have a last chance to inspire their teams to deliver a great performance. So what do top managers and coaches actually say and do?

When trying to give his players the final push towards a great performance, England coach Sven-Göran Eriksson talks to them for five or ten minutes before leaving the hotel. At that stage he focuses on repeating his analysis of the opposition – areas where they have strengths and that the team should look out for, and areas of potential weakness that they can attack.

> 'I talk about our way to play, but it's just for five or ten minutes, and it's more or less a repetition of what we've done during practice. With the national team, when you have them together for two or three days, what you do is try to organize them. There's not a lot of technical work because we don't have time to do that. So the pre-match talk is repetition of what they should already know from practice. Then we go to the stadium, and just before the game starts I say a few words – just what's important. That depends on how I see the players looking. Are they concentrating? Are they white in the face? Are they nervous? So it depends.'

Eriksson believes it important to try to give his players courage, particularly the younger ones, and to remind them they can beat anyone. Why can't we beat Germany?

Former England rugby head coach Clive Woodward didn't go in for rousing team talks before a match.

> *'I'm not big on that at all. I don't think you need a team talk to motivate them. In my playing days the team talk was tribal – about having pride in England. Now before we go out, the England team is very calm and focused. And when they go out onto the pitch there's often ten minutes to go before the start of the game. You don't go blasting out of the changing room. When they go out they're just thinking about the game. We have complete silence for a minute beforehand to think things through. So it's very cool, very calm, just reinforcing one or two key messages. It's all performance based. It's not about winning or about having pride in England. We know all that. We have to keep our thoughts clearly on the first kick off, our first moves, the first tackle, the first offence. You just want to visualize the start of the game.'*

HALF-TIME TALKS

At half-time, managers and coaches get another chance to motivate their players. They have a chance to make tactical adjustments, to point out areas of weakness that need attention and simply to encourage a great effort in the second half.

Just as former England rugby head coach Clive Woodward tried to encourage a sense of cool, calm focus before the start of a match, so coolness and calm is the order of the day at half-time too. Woodward says:

> *'At half-time we have three minutes of silence while the players take on food and put on clean kit. We then split forwards and backs and have three minutes, hopefully being cool and calm, just getting the right points across. We then come together for literally a minute and on a board will be*

three or four points for the team. We just go through those and then we hand over to Johnson, the captain. It's very tempting to walk in and scream and shout, but that's not what it's about.'

England football coach Sven-Göran Eriksson may look calm on the outside, but he admits that he gets upset and disappointed when his team is behind or underperforming. However, at half-time he focuses on what he needs to do to encourage a better result, rather than just venting his own feelings.

'In half-time, if we are behind, you have to be positive. You have to give the players the right advice about what to do in the second half. At half-time I first give the players a few minutes before I start talking, so that they are calm. Then it's important at half-time that you don't talk about everything that happened in the first half, because they can't take it all in. You have to concentrate on two or three important things, which will help to change the performance in the second half. You can't give them ten or fifteen details, because they can't take in that much information.'

Former Ireland manager Jack Charlton agrees that half-time talks require great control from managers if things aren't going well. Charlton says:

'At half-time, on the odd occasion that things aren't going exactly as you want them to, you've really got to bag your tongue before you go into the dressing room; the last thing the players want you to do is to stand there yelling at them at half-time, because nothing will get through to them. You are there to watch the game, see what's happening and explain to the players what's happening and to point out to them what their responsibilities are. If they're not doing their jobs you talk to them, you instruct them. You don't yell at them because no good manager ever got through to anybody by yelling at them. You've got to control that in yourself.'

Charlton did sometimes lose his temper, however. He recalls a match between Ireland and Liechtenstein that Ireland needed to win in order to qualify for the 1996 European championship.

> *'At half-time we could have been winning 5–0, but they were not interested in playing us at all. They just stopped us from scoring and they were doing well at it. At half-time I went into the players and told them we weren't getting at them quick enough; we weren't getting enough people up forward. I was yelling my head off. Andy Townsend [Ireland midfielder] said to me, "Hey boss, it's not like you. Stop what you're doing." I said, "Andy, you're dead right pal." But this was a one-off game that we had to win. But we drew and it cost us qualification into the European championships.*
>
> *'I was upset over the game, but I didn't shout at full-time. It was over then; it was too late. I shouted at half-time – and that did no good whatsoever. The players needed from me to know about how to do what they needed in order to get back into the game, to get a goal back that they needed – that would win them the game. They wanted me to be positive, not negative, which is the way all coaches should be – positive, not negative.'*

Former England Under-21 football coach David Platt has honed his half-time talk techniques over his career.

> *'I made the mistake early on of going in and talking when the physios were still looking at injuries and giving people ice and talking to players. If you do that, you don't get the focus.*
>
> *'Now I usually give the physios a minute or two to look at players. Then I make sure everybody is in and ask if everybody is alright. Then I hit the four serious points that come from the first half. Then I can go round the room on an individual basis to raise other points which revolve around*

an individual or a group of two or three together. But I don't want to lose the effect of the four salient points.'

Platt actually finds it harder to brief the team at half-time when things are going well.

'Those 15 minutes take a long time to pass when you have done well. If you are not doing well there can be more to say. When you have done well you don't change too many things round and you find that you have maybe five or six minutes to kill. Sometimes you can sense a relaxation in the players too.'

The team talk at half-time won't necessarily change the course of a match, but it could do. Delivering a clear-headed, incisive and simple briefing can help to put players back on track to victory – or help them to maintain or even extend a winning lead. Learning to give such team talks is therefore an invaluable skill that any coach or manager can develop.

Analysis V

TEAM SPIRIT

IN PART V WE LOOKED AT THE GROUP EFFORTS that achieve success in the sporting world, whether in team sports or in terms of the supporting personnel around a solo performer.

CHAPTER 17

In Chapter 17: The Right Combination, we looked at the importance of selecting the right individuals to create a successful team.

We found that team selectors look for some of the characteristics we identified earlier in this book as being important for personal success. For example, England football manager Sven-Göran Eriksson looks for players with positive outlooks. Former England rugby head coach Clive Woodward looked for people who are open to new ideas and will try new things. He liked to include players who would learn from each other and try to raise their games to meet the standard that a team-mate set.

When selecting the team captain, different managers may look for different personal characteristics and abilities. Mental strength is always needed, but captains aren't always extroverts. They do have to be respected by their team-mates, however.

Ceri Evans from Gazing Performance says that one of the roles of the captain is to influence the team members in terms of where their attention is placed in pressure situations. Sometimes that involves providing an overview for the team, and sometimes a change of attention is required.

Once the team is picked, it is important to encourage team spirit. Clive Woodward wanted his men to feel elite and special and to create a culture of excellence around them. They also needed to understand and accept the needs and rules of the team.

Team spirit may require you to put the needs of the group ahead of your own, as Roger Black did when deciding the order in which the British 4×400m relay team would run in the 1991 World Championships. By giving up the glory of running the last lap, Black played his part in taking the gold medal away from the American team.

When building support teams, again the creation of a positive, inclusive environment is important. Everyone in the group needs to understand the role they play and understand its importance. As Ron Dennis, boss of the McLaren racing team knows, the driver needs to perform on race day, but he wouldn't even get to the start line without an effective support team.

Applications

- When selecting teams, be clear about what qualities you most value in the team members.

- When appointing a team captain, there is no one type of personality that is necessarily right for the job. Captains can have different personalities – some more extrovert than others – but they must always command the respect of their team-mates.
- Be prepared to accept that the greater good of the team may mean your personal pride has to take second place.
- All team members need to understand and appreciate what other team members contribute to the team result.

CHAPTER 18

In Chapter 18: Team Build-up, we looked at how team members, managers and support staff can work together effectively to create a strong team.

We found that former England rugby head coach Clive Woodward believes in a strong team code. Team members need to accept and buy into the team rules, perhaps even setting the rules themselves. Our interviews certainly showed it was important for all team members to buy into a common set of values and to follow a common vision.

Renzie Hanham from mental conditioning specialists Gazing Performance says that when there is absence of alignment within any group, there will be disharmony, disruption and the potential for diversions. In a group situation it's essential to have clarity and agreement around direction, purpose, goals, roles, responsibilities and the plan that will get you to where you want to go.

The team culture needs to be one where members feel confident and not always worried about making mistakes. The team needs to be strong enough to be able to remain focused on the task in hand, rather than pointing the finger and blaming each other.

Effective communication within the team is vital for creating the right environment. Members need to be understanding of the differences between themselves and others and able to give and accept feedback. This requires an environment of trust and mutual respect.

278 MIND GAMES ▶▶▶

Ceri Evans from mental conditioning specialists Gazing Performance says that strong teams are made up of strong individuals. Everyone should be able to express themselves, so long as that self-expression supports the team structure and goals.

The challenge in team sports is to bring each individual to the peak of their own performance at the right time. This requires each team member to prepare thoroughly, not only in terms of physical training but also in thinking about how to beat the opposition – analysing their strengths and weaknesses.

Team members also need the ability to be able to move their attention between focusing on their own processes and focusing on the wider field of play – considering where the other players are and what would be an effective team move. The Gazing Performance approach talks about the 'gazing principle' – the deliberate movement of attention between an overview and the detail. As Ceri Evans from Gazing Performance explains, at times you need to focus on detail, but at other times you also need an overview to be effective. Influential players in rugby, for example, need to know where other people are. They need a sense of the wider space as well as a sense of their own position. They need to attend to their own particular tasks while also being aware of the bigger picture. It is the deliberate movement between the overview and the detail that's critical. The same applies in business, Evans says. Effectiveness can be improved by having an awareness of the overall framework one is working within, and the specific task or process at hand. For example, a salesperson trying to make a sale will be helped by placing their attention on the specifics of the selling process. However, they may also be assisted by maintaining an overview of the whole process, and where the current interaction sits within the larger scheme of things. This involves an interplay between guiding principles and practical detail. Both are needed; one without the other is less effective.

During extended competitions, it is important that team members can relax sufficiently. They need to be able to cope with boredom, too. When staying away from home, creating a sense of familiarity around the team camp is also important. It is crucial that coaches and managers ensure the team feels well-cared for and comfortable.

Effective teams understand their strategic play, and how to work with each other to maximum effect. Sometimes learning new patterns of play can be difficult. Jack Charlton, when manager at Middlesbrough, found it took time and constant repetition of instructions to get his players to act as he wanted in the heat of a game.

Applications

- If you are a team coach or manager, you need to provide clear direction to your team members.
- Team spirit requires everyone to accept the team's values and rules. Encourage team members to play a part in setting team rules to encourage compliance with them. Peer pressure is an important element in encouraging positive behaviour.
- Encourage a supportive team culture where members feel confident about taking decisions under pressure. Coaches and managers can help to do this by developing an atmosphere that avoids apportioning blame.
- Think about how team members communicate with each other. Encourage the sharing of ideas and thoughts about how to improve team performance, but without direct criticism of individual players. You want to try to develop an atmosphere of trust and mutual support.
- Encourage team members to practise moving the focus of their attention from their own performance and processes to that of the team. Encouraging this movement between the narrow and the wide focus helps individuals to understand how their role impacts on others, and how to perform it most effectively.
- Think about how you can help your team relax but remain focused on the task in hand during extended competitive situations.

- Allow time for repetitive drilling of new team manoeuvres or procedures to give team members the chance to learn them properly.

CHAPTER 19

The final moments before competition begins are important for team success. In Chapter 19: Team Talks, we looked at how captains, coaches and managers can try to send out their teams in the best possible frame of mind.

The captain's role is important, but one that varies depending on the individual involved. Former Australian rugby captain Michael Lynagh would walk around the dressing room talking quietly to team members. He didn't find he needed to give big motivational talks. Captains with different personalities, however, can say some inspirational words to the whole team if they like. The right approach depends on the personalities involved.

Coaches and managers will have briefed their players thoroughly by the morning of competition. They make sure they don't overload their players with extra information or new instructions late in the pre-match preparation. England football manager Sven-Göran Eriksson speaks to the team for just five or ten minutes before they leave their hotel on the way to a game. He briefly repeats his analysis of the opposition and its strengths and weaknesses. Just before the game starts he again says just a few words, chosen in response to the mood he sees in his players. Above all, he aims to give them courage.

Former England rugby head coach Clive Woodward also tried to keep things simple on the day of a game. He gave players a small number of key points for them to concentrate on. Again like Eriksson, he didn't go in for rousing team talks before a match. He knew his players were already motivated to do their best.

At half-time again the top coaches and managers understand the importance of not overloading their team players with too much information. Woodward hones in on just a few points to remember when play recommences. Top coaches and managers also realize that players need time to refresh themselves, change their kit or see to any niggling potential injuries.

Ceri Evans from mental conditioning specialists Gazing Performance says that if you want to change the way things are going, you need to influence the attention of the individual or the whole team as a group. There is a danger in overloading them with information. If people are performing under pressure, you need to give them simple, clear messages. It is not possible for people to effectively place their attention on multiple things at the same time. If it is felt to be necessary to give more than two or three pieces of information or direction, it is more practical to give specific advice to sections of the team. You can link a phase of play to a certain thing they should think about. Keep it to a few messages, otherwise the players get overloaded.

Managers believe it is important that they try to retain a cool head. Shouting at players, even if their play has been frustrating, is not considered generally the most effective way to improve the second-half performance. This isn't easy, as Jack Charlton sometimes found when managing Ireland's national football squad. However, when he did let off steam, he found it didn't help the players, or the result, at all.

The one time shouting can be helpful is if a player has got stuck in some unhelpful state. Renzie Hanham from Gazing Performance, says shouting can be used to break that state. If someone is in a state of inertia, numbness or indifference, shouting can disturb it and start getting them back to focusing on some meaningful processes.

As ever, coaches and managers have to use their experience and judgement to determine the appropriate response in the circumstances they currently face.

Applications

- If you are a captain, remain true to your own personality. Introverts do not need to give rousing speeches before a match if this is not natural to their temperament. Quiet, personal encouragement to individual team members can be as effective.

- Coaches or managers should not overload team members with information at the last minute. If you are coaching or managing a team, try to keep final briefings highly focused. Give people a few key points to concentrate on.
- In the middle of a match, competition or any other extended event, coaches can help to put teams back on track. Again success lies in not overwhelming team members with detail. Focus on what individuals or sections in the team need to do to raise their performance.
- Coaches and team managers should try not to lose their cool in the heat of the moment. Shouting at teams and individuals will not usually generate improved performance. It is far better to speak calmly and maintain your own focus on the task in hand – briefing the team effectively.

INDEX

Printed and bound in the UK by
CPI Antony Rowe, Eastbourne

Printed and bound by CPI Group (UK) Ltd, Croydon, CR0 4YY

29/11/2022

03167358-0001